the jubilee line extension

the jubilee line extension

kenneth powell

foreword by roland paoletti

laurence king

Published in 2000
by Laurence King Publishing
an imprint of Calmann & King Ltd
71 Great Russell Street
London WC1B 3BN
Tel: +44 20 7831 6351
Fax: +44 20 7831 8356

e-mail: enquiries@calmann-king.co.uk
www.laurence-king.com

This book was produced by Calmann & King
Ltd in association with the London Transport
Museum

A catalogue record for this book is available
from the British Library.

ISBN 1 85669 184 5

Designed by Isambard Thomas
Picture research by Mary-Jane Gibson
Specially commissioned photography
by Dennis Gilbert and Timothy Soar

Printed in Italy

Title page: Staircase detail at Southwark
Station (photo: Peter Durant/arcblue.com)

foreword

'I should call an architect one who is able with sound and marvellous order and reason – both with his mind and heart to conceive, and with his work to carry out all things which – by means of the movements of weights and the joining and amassing of bodies – can with the greatest dignity be fitted to the uses of men. And to do this he must know things of passing excellence, and have mastered them.'

In 1960, when I was studying in Venice, a teacher, Ernesto Rogers, an uncle of Richard Rogers, commended Alberti's 500-year-old definition of an architect as one that has never been bettered. In turn the great engineer Pier Luigi Nervi, with whom I worked for several years in Rome, would also refer to it from time to time. In 1990, on my arrival from Hong Kong, I pinned the dictum above my desk. Half a millennium after its writing, nothing could more graphically describe the architectural and engineering initiative of the Jubilee Line Extension.

The Jubilee Line Extension has a maintenance depot, a control centre and eleven stations: Westminster, Waterloo, Southwark, London Bridge, Bermondsey, Canada Water, Canary Wharf, North Greenwich, Canning Town, West Ham and Stratford. Nine of the eleven are interchanges, making this the only line on the Underground to connect to all existing lines. Four of the stations have large new bus stations attached.

The route and stations of the extension effectively link Victorian construction with the modern world and propel both into the future. While the Jubilee Line ticket halls have been carved out of the vast nineteenth-century vaulted under-crofts of London Bridge and Waterloo main line stations, new stations have been built to advanced architectural concepts.

From the outset Chairman Sir Wilfrid Newton and Managing Director (later Chief Executive) Denis Tunnicliffe were fully agreed that the new extension should be based on the latest technology. As an extension of an existing line there is a limit to what can be achieved, but emphasis for the new stations was for more modern space accommodating much improved escalator and escape provisions.

This sentiment led to their early support for the use of architects to lead the design strategy for stations, though it was firmly expected that following the Hong Kong precedent a single unified theme would be developed for all stations on the basis of conventional civil engineering solutions. Before I left Hong Kong, however, I had already resolved to propose otherwise and after some months of delay this was agreed. In short, the proposal was that each of the eleven stations of the extension should be designed as an individual entity, but linked to the others by an underlying philosophy and essential elements. Each should be unique and should contribute strongly to its neighbourhood while at the same time representing recognisably the best of London Underground. Some stations should have more money spent on them than others. A different London architect should be chosen for each station and the depot.

There were solid philosophic and practical reasons for spreading the load. A single architect would be too vulnerable and tend to iron things out. At the best of times circumstances make the good planning of underground stations very difficult to achieve and it takes a lot of stamina to get there. In this case, in the very short time that we had given ourselves to produce drawings for construction, it would have been difficult to achieve the high results and the differentiations I was after without the use of a number of architects.

In 1990 the response from architects to advertisements for engineering and architectural consultants interested in designing the extension and its stations was both sparse and disappointing. In spite of the fact that there was a deep recession and little architectural work about, there was no reaction. The extension of a 1970s underground line which itself had been cobbled together from older lines across 10 unprepossessing miles of south-east and east London was simply not an interesting proposal for the architectural profession. Moreover, visits to and talks with many architects exposed their further doubts, which were partly to do with civil engineering management and partly with the architecture of earlier tube lines. Nevertheless, the intrinsic potential of the extension was explained to them and they were told that if they were not able to help then it really would be the end as far as authentic architecture and the underground railway was concerned.

A limited competitive and prequalification system was then established and Ian Ritchie and the late Ron Herron were the first architects to be brought into the project. As a result curiosity was aroused and the project's status enhanced. Slowly others of the same calibre followed and a team was chosen: Chris Wilkinson; Troughton McAslan; Alsop Lyall & Störmer; Norman Foster; Herron Associates; Eva Jiricna; Ian Ritchie; Richard MacCormac; Weston Williamson; Michael Hopkins; Michael Manser and Arup Associates were signed up, with the project's in-house architects being brought in to design Waterloo and the plans for London Bridge. Some of the practices were small and less well known, some have since become famous through the Jubilee Line. When approached Will Alsop had not yet won his great commission in Marseilles. The more renowned practices remained reluctant and required much persuading to join, but once aboard performed wonders, as did Norman Foster who was pro-active from the start.

Preference was not given to 'transport' architects, as to do so would have excluded many of the most capable architects in the metropolis. No architect was selected on reputation alone. Like-minded architects were sought who, it was thought, would do the job well and possessed a talent for understanding engineering. In short, they were chosen as a loose team with strong characteristics stemming from a common enthusiasm for and a knowledge of engineering and, individually, an aptitude for resolution of the problems particular to each station.

In my experience, underground engineers either provide the spatial layouts themselves or all too easily take on board pliable designers with whom they feel comfortable and this all too often produces labyrinthine tunnels and ad hoc formless space, usually encrusted with some mild decoration as a palliative. By contrast, on the Jubilee Line extension an open-minded commissioning policy – allowing free rein to some of the country's best architects to work on the stations in their entirety, from street to platform levels – has been rewarded with a highly functional series of bold and intelligent designs.

When publicised in September 1992 the designs, and the choice of architects, met with general approval. The Royal Fine Arts Commission praised the project as 'an example of patronage at its best and most enlightened and [we] congratulate London Transport for its inspired efforts which recall the remarkable pre-war achievements of the Underground under the leadership of Frank Pick'.

Together with the concept of achieving a symbiosis of architecture and engineering – with daylight itself used as a structuring and directional device – the design priorities were to provide generous and easily understood space, clear and direct passenger routing, a sufficiency of escalators (a total of 118 increasing the number in the network by over 40 per cent), lifts for the disabled and safety in all its aspects, particularly by the provision of protected escape routes. Priority was given to providing the above elements – which can never be introduced once a station is built – rather than elaborate finishes. Indeed instruction was given to leave civil work exposed wherever possible – to undecorate rather than decorate the station.

In the end, the architects' considerable contribution has been a re-examination of what engineers do in an effort to return to the origins of engineering. They have defined space and reinvented it.

For generations the Underground's infrastructural engineering was locked in an unbreakable pattern of unchanging and unchangeable solutions. But what the Jubilee Line managed to do was to create a situation and allow heavy engineering, which was so often static and inhuman, to become instead resourceful and brilliant and active in response to architectural initiatives.

On the completion of the Extension, Denis Tunnicliffe recalled: 'Immediately I was captured by the vision, and became passionate to deliver it, and the brilliant feats of integrated architecture, design and engineering which are its most visible expression – I can't say that I had a huge interest in architecture before my involvement with the Extension but I always had a feel for design. It didn't take much, then, for Roland to persuade me against the Holden-knew-best tendency, and their quest for continuity. We wanted a design vocabulary that looked forward, not back. And we had, for the first time in the history of London Underground, the luxury of space and the opportunity to do the job properly; that's why the architecture is assertive, why the Extension stations' heroic aesthetics match fitness for purpose, why, in short, they are a great expression of confidence in the future. Our stations are big enough to accommodate the needs of Londoners for the next 100 years. In all this innovation, there is also a profound continuity. The Extension shows, as so often in the past, that the Underground can power the re-shaping and revitalisation of our great city like no other force'.

A few days later a columnist in The Spectator wrote: 'The Jubilee Line Extension stations have everything – elegance, gravitas and sense of purpose'. Later the diarist went on to say, 'perhaps it is the unfathomable nature of the Dome that makes people generally fonder of the Ferris Wheel. The Wheel is what you see. It is without politics and blithely without education. However, the most popular millennium sight of all has turned out to be … Canary Wharf tube station. It has really caught the public imagination. And everybody can afford the tickets. This is the true people's building'.

Roland Paoletti
March 2000

1

introduction

The Underground is part of the Londoner's birthright and something that anyone who comes to live in London soon takes for granted, bemoans, but also cares about and even has a certain affection for. It is more than 125 years since the beginnings of a revolution in travel, when the first steam trains ran below the streets of London. The Underground forms a continuing sequence, in which the Jubilee Line Extension (JLE) is the latest chapter.

The railway made modern London. Early Victorian London was a tightly packed hive of rich and poor, the latter concentrated in areas – the Strand, Covent Garden, the South Bank, the City fringes – which are now part of the commercial and public heart of the capital. The slums had to be cleared in the interests of hygiene and municipal progress – the Metropolitan Line and Holborn Viaduct at Farringdon displaced the 4,000 people who were crammed into the 348 houses which came down. These people had to go somewhere. Cheap trains into the mainline termini, linked by the Inner Circle (now Circle Line) was part of the answer. From the 1870s on, the new working-class suburbs – immortalized as Mr Pooter-land by G. and W. Grossmith in *The Diary of a Nobody* – mopped up many of the displaced. By the end of the century, trams run by the London County Council provided a new means of affordable transport, their routes forming a new map of the metropolis. The last tram vanished half a century ago, although they may yet return. But the 'tube' goes on. Its role in redefining the map of London is an active one, as the JLE will prove. The Underground created whole new areas of London – South Kensington (once Brompton) and Clapham South (part of Battersea), for example. To live outside the radius of the Underground is, for many Londoners, to live beyond the pale.

By 1918, visitors to London were advised to make use of the 'elaborate system of underground electric railways, with frequent trains, providing a cheap and rapid form of transit'. The Danish architect Steen Eiler Rasmussen (who first came to London in 1927) famously commented: 'The only true modern construction is, taken as a whole, not architecture. [The Underground] is more important for London than all the works of Lutyens and England's other famous architects put together.'[1]

By the 1920s, the essential framework of the Underground was firmly in place, with the tubes constructed between 1890 and 1907 and unified as a system by C.T. Yerkes. The routes adopted were partly dictated by the perceived market, but also by the geography and geology of London. The tunnelling technology, which derived from that developed by Marc Isambard and Isambard Kingdom Brunel for the pioneering Thames Tunnel (opened in 1843 after 18 years' work) worked well in the dense London clay. But the history of the Brunels' scheme underlined the problems in tunnelling through the waterlogged sand and gravel of the docklands – a key engineering achievement of the JLE. Until the advent of the JLE, the tube's impact on South London was limited to the bold intervention of the Northern Line.

The Underground was about engineering. Was architecture, as Rasmussen implied, irrelevant to its operations? The same issue had been addressed by the builders of mainline railways from the 1830s onwards and answered in the negative. To the irritation of a later generation of supposed 'functionalists', railway architecture developed not just as an expression of practical needs but as a statement about the public role of the railway in the Victorian city. At

St Pancras Station of 1865–8, art and engineering were fused not just in the train-shed (by engineers W.H. Barlow & R.M. Ordish), a great iron and glass span sitting on huge brick vaults, but also in Sir George Gilbert Scott's Grand Hotel of 1868–74, where Gothic ornament was combined with extensive use of iron construction.

As soon as the Underground became a unified system, it began to develop a uniform architectural expression with the first 40 or so stations designed by Leslie Green in the 1900s, many still extant and characterized by the use of a Classical kit of parts, executed in glazed faience on a steel frame. The idea of a coherent Underground architecture was born. It was part of '…the myth of the London Underground, the image of the coherent, patriarchal, beneficent, civic-minded system of public transport for Londoners', promoted by Frank Pick, director of the London Passenger Transport Board between the mid-1920s and the Second World War. [2] Pick's favourite architectural collaborator was Charles Holden (other practices also received commissions). Holden's name has become indelibly associated with the Underground. On the Morden extension of the Northern Line (1923–6) his role was confined to designing the Classical ticket hall blocks – the architecture did not extend beyond the escalators. The architecture, said Pick, 'neither apes the past nor undermines modernity by violating taste'. With the surface stations on the Piccadilly Line, such as Sudbury Town (1931) and Arnos Grove (1932), Holden's supervision extended to detailing platforms, lighting, seats and such like. Influenced by contemporary Dutch and Scandinavian building, Holden created a modern architecture which, while rooted in Classical traditions, eschewed the rhetoric of the Modern Movement.

The original Paddington Station (1868, now demolished) was typical of the first era of Underground architecture, a dignified adjunct to Brunel's mainline terminal.

By the 1900s, with the work of Leslie Green – as at Chalk Farm – a distinctive neoclassical Underground architecture had emerged.

Nikolaus Pevsner, writing in 1943, described Holden's approach as 'serviceable, uncompromisingly modern, and yet in keeping with the quiet distinction of the Georgian brick house.'[3] The Holden manner has become identified with a particularly British approach to modernity – it is sensible, cautious and moderate – though it was part of a school of modern traditionalism which flourished not only in the Netherlands and Sweden but equally in Nazi Germany and Fascist Italy. Holden's stations became icons and the universalism of the Holden/Pick alliance provided a foundation, in theory at least, for London Transport's design philosophy up until the construction of the Victoria Line in the 1960s – the last scheme by Holden's practice was completed as late as 1961. Significantly, the Holden legacy held no sway with JLE Architect in Charge, Roland Paoletti. The JLE project was inevitably compared to the building programme of the inter-war years, though some critics questioned the decision to use a variety of architects, which encouraged diversity rather than uniformity.

The Victoria Line, begun in 1962 and completed in 1971, was strategically a major gain to London's transport system, especially for its fast links between the termini of King's Cross, St Pancras, Euston and Victoria, and the West End. In design terms, the project was dominated by a dry modernism imposed by consultant Misha Black of the Design Research Unit (DRU), an industrial design organization which advised London Transport until the early 1980s. There was only one new surface station (Blackhorse Road of 1968) and that was unremarkable. Black commented: 'The stations may be criticized for appearing visually unexciting, but we consider that preferable to a transient popularity without lasting qualities.'[4]

In the absence of any new lines, Underground architecture during the 1970s and 1980s consisted of the refurbishment and restyling of existing stations. Despite the reverence for Holden and Pick, damaging alterations were carried out to some of their stations and the resulting controversy led to the listing of dozens of stations. (Some of the best Holden stations had been listed as early as 1971 and by 1994 there were nearly 50 listed Underground stations.) London Transport seemed to be searching for a new identity and graphics were a key feature. Printed metal panels, ornamental tiles, plastics and even mosaic – as seen in Sir Eduardo Paolozzi's work, commissioned in 1979 at Tottenham Court Road – were used to cheer up well-worn stations. Claddings and finishes were in favour, the purism of the DRU years having been abandoned. The King's Cross fire of 1987, which killed 31 people, brought about an abrupt reversal of policy. By 1990 London Underground design strategy aimed to '... create a calming visual environment of neutral colours and rationalized signage ...' There was a recognition that stations needed to be intelligible, lighter and more spacious, leaving behind the confined spaces in which the King's Cross tragedy had occurred. There is no doubt this affected the company response to Paoletti's proposals for the JLE. Up until then the few new stations of the early 1990s were transitional in their approach rather than innovative. The new Angel Station on the Northern Line, located beneath a big office development, was distinguished by its exceptionally long escalator run and by spacious platforms and lower-level concourse spaces, contrived by digging a new northbound tunnel. The ticket hall is purely functional. At Hillingdon, where the old, 1930s-built station was demolished for road improvements, the chosen

The architectural input of Charles Holden extended no further below ground than the escalators – here (at Clapham South) given a striking lighting scheme.

Holden's surface stations on the Piccadilly Line, including Sudbury Town (1931), were remarkable for their stripped Classical booking hall and platform blocks.

opposite
The booking hall at Sudbury Town is one of Holden's finest works – a dignified civic space for a growing suburban area.

architectural vocabulary was lightweight steel and glass. The rebuilt Hammersmith was superficially high-tech in manner, but with memories of Holden's streamlining. In all these stations, the bright graphics of the past were suppressed in favour of rather bland, all-white finishes.

The Jubilee Line between Stanmore and Charing Cross involved limited new construction since it took over the former Stanmore branch of the Bakerloo Line. The new section from Baker Street to Charing Cross was seen as phase I of the proposed Fleet Line, which had been under consideration since the war years. From Charing Cross, the Fleet Line was to run via the Aldwych and through the City to Fenchurch Street, then through the Brunels' Thames Tunnel, taking over the New Cross branch of the East London Line and extending to Lewisham. The Jubilee Line opened in 1979. A year earlier there had been an official start on what was effectively the Jubilee Line Extension east of Charing Cross, though it was now known as the River Line and projected to run via the Isle of Dogs and Royal Docks to the Greater London Council's 'new town' at Thamesmead. Work soon ground to a halt, however, and it was not until 1993 that London Underground began constructing the JLE.

The project had been resuscitated because of the renaissance of the former docklands – the last working dock closed in 1981 – as a new business and residential quarter and, in particular, the construction of the flagship development at Canary Wharf in the Isle of Dogs. Margaret Thatcher's government established the London Docklands Development Corporation (LDDC) in 1981 with plenary planning and development powers over 2,000 hectares (5,000 acres) of the old docklands. The Canary Wharf project – 800,000

In the late 1960s and early 1970s only a limited tile decoration scheme was permitted on the Victoria Line, but by the early 1980s the ornately decorative mosaics created by Eduardo Paolozzi for Tottenham Court Road Station (bottom) were followed by other decorative schemes in West End stations.

opposite
Underground architecture of the 1990s has ranged from the fanciful steel canopies at Hammersmith (top) to the emphasis on clarity and simplicity at Angel (bottom).

square metres (8.8 million square feet) of offices and up to 40,000 jobs – surfaced in 1985 under the aegis of developer G. Ware Travelstead and was rapidly given planning consent by the LDDC, despite opposition from community groups and Labour-controlled local authorities. After Olympia & York (O&Y) took over as developers in 1987, construction finally started on the site of the old West India Docks. Among the massive public subsidies poured into the project was an extension of the Docklands Light Railway to Bank Station, opened in 1991, together with a large new station at Canary Wharf, designed by Cesar Pelli (as was the central 243-metre/800-foot tower of the development). O&Y paid only 40 per cent of the £280 million cost, but still wanted a fast rail connection from Waterloo. London Transport was adamantly opposed to a stand-alone line with few benefits for the rest of London. Its view was supported by the East London Rail Study of 1989. Finally, the principle of building the JLE from Waterloo to Stratford via Docklands was confirmed, though there were still decisions to be made about the detailed route of the line and the Greenwich peninsula was for a time bypassed. O&Y were to contribute £400 million to the cost. In return, they were given a considerable say in the design of the Canary Wharf station. Their first instinct was to have it designed by an American architectural practice, possibly that of Cesar Pelli. It was the inability to pay an initial sum of £40 million to the JLE which led to the financial collapse of O&Y in 1992. Canary Wharf's contribution to the JLE was subsequently rescheduled and, in effect, greatly reduced. On this basis, John Major's government gave the green light for the project to start late in 1993. One City analyst has argued that Canary Wharf is 'a sort of

concrete Eurofighter', which has enjoyed up to £1 billion of public subsidy: '... as a monument to non-intervention by government, it will always raise a laugh ...'[5] Canary Wharf has been portrayed as a Thatcherite monument, yet it embodies principles alien to the Thatcher government's free-market agenda.

The parliamentary bill for the JLE, which allowed the project to bypass most normal planning controls, was deposited in 1989 and finally passed in 1992. The parliamentary process provided an opportunity for aspects of the project to be reassessed: the idea of a new Westminster Station in Parliament Square, for example, was ruled out; the routing via North Greenwich was confirmed; and the form of Canning Town Station laid down. The case for the line in cost/benefit terms had to be established. But the broad social and economic case for the line emerged only after construction had begun – the plans for the Millennium Festival at Greenwich and the major regeneration focus on Stratford reinforced the case, while Southwark, which benefits particularly from the JLE, is emerging, thanks to Bankside's Tate Modern and other developments, as the most dynamic London borough of the millennium. The late 1990s emphasis on brownfield development (the regeneration of redundant land within towns or industrial zones) further strengthened the case for regenerating inner-London.

These developments were part of a redrawing of the map of London. Whatever the merits or otherwise of Canary Wharf, it did pull investment eastwards from the City and underpinned politician Michael Heseltine's East Thames Corridor initiative. Confirmation in 1998 that the Channel Tunnel Rail Link would go to Stratford was another significant landmark. Old preconceptions about

the character of areas like Stratford, Canning Town and Bermondsey were challenged and all were now firmly on the map of London. The architectural agenda of the JLE was also set to challenge preconceptions and to celebrate the dynamic diversity of twenty-first-century London. The key image of the Holden/Pick era had been of a new suburban station set among newly completed semi-detached houses with countryside in the background – the Underground as the uniting force for a fast-growing, suburbanized metropolis. The corresponding image of the JLE may be represented in Bermondsey or Canning Town Stations, symbols of London's rediscovery of itself and, arguably, of London Underground's recognition that a great tradition needs to be regularly renewed if it is not to become a dead shibboleth.

Notes

1 Andrew Saint, 'What the Underground means for London' in *Rassegna*, London Underground, 66 (1996) ed. S. Brandolini, p. 24.

2 *op. cit.*, p. 29.

3 Nikolaus Pevsner, *An Outline of European Architecture* (revised edition), (Harmondsworth 1945), p. 218.

4 Quoted in D. Lawrence, *Underground Architecture* (Harrow 1994), p. 168.

5 Christopher Fildes in the *Daily Telegraph*, 6 March 1999.

For the planning history of the JLE, see Jon Willis, *Extending the Jubilee Line* (London Transport 1997).

For a critical history of the LDDC and Canary Wharf, see Peter Hall, *Cities in Civilisation* (London 1998), pp. 888–931.

2

the stations

westminster

For countless tourists, the most potent symbol of London is Westminster's Big Ben, a vertical icon as memorable as New York's Empire State Building or Paris' Eiffel Tower. At the height of the season, visitors throng the streets around Parliament Square, surprised perhaps that the latter is a barely accessible lawn surrounded by traffic, rather than a real public space, but conscious that they are close to great events, past and present. For a thousand years, Westminster Abbey and the Palace of Westminster have been a focus of national life. For the builders of the JLE, constructing a new station in this place was one of the greatest challenges they faced on the line.

The origins of the Abbey are obscure, but it became a significant centre of religious life under Edward the Confessor in the eleventh century. King Edward's abbey (rebuilt for Henry III in 1245) rose on an island in the muddy reaches of the Thames and alongside it the king (later canonized) built a new royal palace. The monastery was dissolved by Henry VIII and the palace evolved into the seat of Parliament, but the symbolism of the place – the union of church and state, the trappings of a constitutional monarchy and a British emphasis on continuity and tradition – remained (and remain) strong. This is hallowed ground, where any new development is subjected to intense scrutiny. Building the new JLE station meant confronting major planning issues as well as practical problems relating to the confined nature of the site.

The Underground had, of course, come close to the precincts of the Palace and Abbey in Victorian times, with a station (opened in 1868) on the Inner Circle, which formed the nucleus of the whole system. This was an open-top station, sunk below a city block and was distinctly unimpressive. A JLE station at Westminster was considered vital, not just as the line's only central London interchange with the District and Circle Lines, but equally as a new gateway to the parliamentary building and the Abbey.

Michael Hopkins and Partners' involvement with the project began in 1989, when the practice won the commission to build an extension to the Palace of Westminster on the corner of Bridge Street and Victoria Embankment. Consisting mostly of offices for MPs, with some committee rooms and administrative accommodation, the New Parliamentary Building (as it became known) was potentially controversial – earlier schemes had been abandoned on the grounds of cost and their intrusive impact on the area. The existence of the District and Circle Line platforms, running diagonally across the site and to remain in use throughout any building project, further complicated the task. Some of the existing buildings were protected by listing and the Hopkins team looked seriously at the possibility of refurbishment rather than total redevelopment, but none of the possible options gave Parliament the space it needed. Nor was it easy to meet London Transport's brief: to provide the key link in a 'campus' of parliamentary buildings between Whitehall and the river. The passage of the JLE's parliamentary bill 'opened up' this apparently intractable site, not least by providing means to bypass normal planning controls and demolish the (not especially distinguished) listed buildings.

The need for a JLE station at Westminster was initially questioned by MPs: St James's Park was suggested as an alternative, but ruled out on technical and strategic grounds, and there were suggestions that the line might run via Embankment or Temple to Waterloo. Even when the principle was accepted, the idea of locating the ticket hall under Parliament Square – clear of buildings and therefore a logical place to put it – was not looked upon favourably. The next best, and most obvious, solution was to combine the station with the parliamentary extension. Hopkins and Partners were eventually selected in 1991, and the two projects were subsequently developed in tandem.

The advent of the JLE resolved major problems – incorporating the existing platforms, for example, had wreaked havoc with floor levels in the new building. The strategy for the site enabled the new station to be built in a deep box, excavated around the existing District Line platforms, with the JLE tracks running one above the other just outside the box. This arrangement, in conjunction with compensation grouting (see page 202), was designed to minimize the potential impact of settlement on Big Ben and the footings of Westminster Bridge. The District and Circle Line tracks were to be lowered by around 300mm (1 foot), just enough to provide adequate headroom in the new ticket hall, sandwiched between the old platforms and the central court of the new development above (where structural loadings were lightest and a wide span could be achieved). This was an enormously laborious operation achieved, a few millimetres at a time, during the brief hours that the system was closed. The floors of MPs' offices above are largely supported by deep foundations extending down through the new station at six points – locating the columns was made more difficult because of the complex interface between the diagonal geometry of the District and Circle Line platforms (with ticket hall above) and the orthogonal form of the subterranean box.

The architects' response to the brief was to display and to celebrate the 'awesome' engineering of the new station, but in truth, the architecture *is* the engineering. From the street, the station reads only as an opening from the pavement in the highly modelled facade of the New Parliamentary Building. Nothing of the former station remains. The new ticket hall is large, superficially matter-of-fact, and far from lofty – indeed, the exposed coffers of the massive *in situ* concrete roof grid, a structure that is essentially practical but with a touch of Nerviesque poetry, provides much needed headroom. The real magic is experienced as the passenger descends, past the reconstructed District and Circle Line platforms, to the JLE.

At Westminster, the JLE is 32 metres (104 feet) below ground level and the site of the station is closely hemmed in by streets and buildings. The diaphragm walls of the station box, 39 metres (127 feet) deep in total, had to be constructed before the central space was excavated – deep trenches were dug into the London clay around the perimeter and infilled with concrete, so that the completed 1 metre- (3 feet-) thick walls bear the mark of the earth in which they were formed. The next stage was to excavate the box from the top, bracing the side walls with horizontal steel props. The shores sit in a supporting system of fair-faced concrete walling beams and vertical buttresses applied to the exposed diaphragm in a rectangular grid. Gradually, a vast subterranean atrium emerged, designed to contain the banks of escalators serving the JLE – the 'engine room' of the station.

There is a striking contrast between the diaphragm walls of the escalator box, formed in the earth and left largely exposed, and the finely finished structure constructed within them. It was not possible to control every detail and finish of the basic engineering (the diaphragm walls and concrete support system), so the architects decided to make a virtue out of necessity, even taking a certain delight in the imperfections of this bold approach. In contrast to new Underground stations of the recent past, but in line with JLE philosophy, applied finishes are kept to a minimum. Architecture is substance, not a skin. The nature of materials is celebrated, and the aesthetic throughout is deliberately muted and neutral: silvery concrete (the mix specified by the architects to create a reflective appearance) and the sheen of stainless steel create the mood. Lighting and controlled use of advertising will provide brightness and colour, while decoration has been totally eschewed. But the station comes to life, like a great machine (which it is), only when the 17 escalators begin to operate, threading their way in scissor formations through the structure of the station.

The diameter of the platform tunnels was kept relatively tight (at 7 metres/22 feet) to protect adjoining buildings, and they are formed with structural cast-iron tunnel rings (rarely used since the nineteenth century) and infilled by perforated acoustic panels above the platforms. The tunnels are the *raison d'être* of the whole structure, yet the drama is elsewhere, on the route from the entry gates to the doors of the train. The escalator box in particular is a perfect marriage of civil engineering and architecture, a clear expression of the central theme that Roland Paoletti sought to infuse into the JLE. The structure communicates the force of the earth bearing in on the box.

Westminster Station has been described, almost inevitably, as Piranesian, yet the adjective implies heaviness, monumentality and a drama rooted in contrasts of darkness and light. The engineering achievement at Westminster is heroic, yet the resulting structural expression is neither overbearing nor contrived, but elegant, economical and surprisingly lightweight. Structurally, the station is a unity with Portcullis House above. Building it, on a tightly constricted site, with a national icon, Big Ben, yards away, was a massive challenge. Working in one of the most sensitive locations in Britain, with Parliament itself as the client, Michael Hopkins and Partners produced a design which is, in the tradition of the practice's recent work, clearly contextual – with obvious references to Norman Shaw's New Scotland Yard next door – if a little overwrought. (The progressive environmental design of the building reflects another strength of the Hopkins office.) Portcullis House is an expression of the taste of the British establishment: modern, yet cautious nonetheless. The station has no time for mannerisms – it is direct, functional (in the best sense) and awe-inspiring. It is this station, says Roland Paoletti, which most fully realizes the potential of the project. At the end of the line from the East, the JLE has achieved its supreme architectural expression. Ideally, it is a point of arrival: the gradual ascent from the westbound JLE platform to the street is one of the great architectural experiences of London. Here architecture and engineering merge to create a timeless spatial entity.

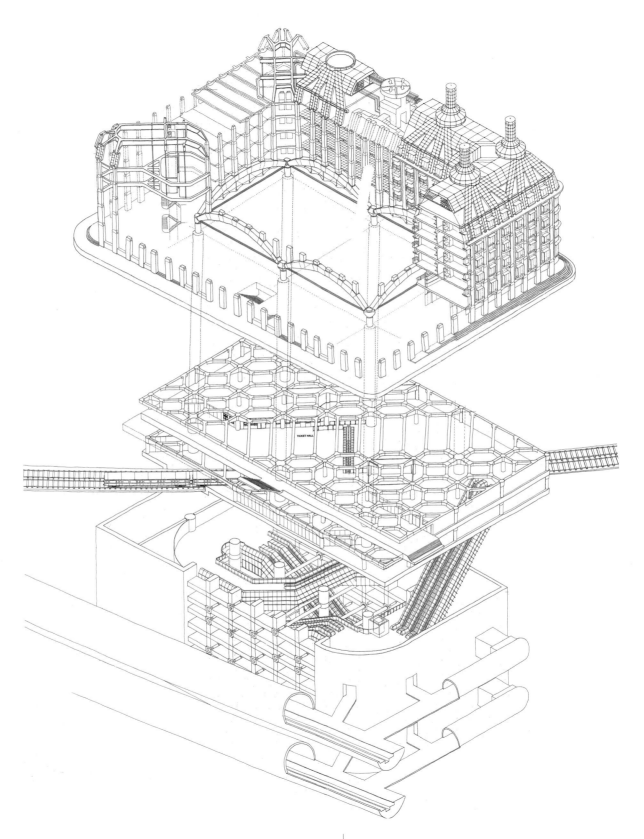

above right
In the shadow of Big Ben, workers construct the Metropolitan District Railway. Westminster's first Underground station opened in 1868.

below right
The station incorporated the existing District and Circle Line tracks, which had to be kept in operation throughout the construction process.

opposite
At Westminster, the new station had to be shoehorned into a tight site yards from Big Ben and was structurally a unity with the new parliamentary building, Portcullis House, which sits on top of the station box and was also designed by Michael Hopkins and Partners.

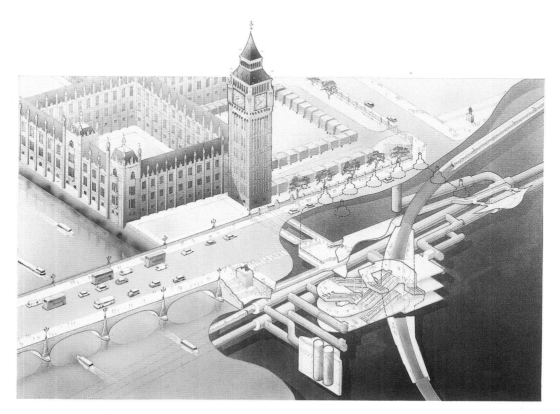

The booking hall is a relatively low space, but is given drama by the frank and poetic expression of structure.

The incomparable impact of Westminster Station is experienced in the 40 metre (130 foot) deep station box, a container for banks of escalators with no extraneous elements.

The relative narrowness of the platform tunnels at Westminster (platform width for all the stations was imposed in the parliamentary bill) forms a counterpoint to the vast spaces of the escalator hall beyond.

waterloo

At Waterloo, as at London Bridge, the JLE's own architectural team led by Sui Te Wu (which was responsible for the station project from first concept to completion) faced the problems of working within the context of an existing rail terminal – London's busiest, handling commuter, long-distance and international traffic. Waterloo, a hub of the Underground system, with connections to the City and West End via the Bakerloo, Northern and Waterloo and City lines, was seen as a vital link in the JLE. What has been achieved there seems deceptively simple, yet it is the outcome of an incisive analysis of the hugely complex site carried through into a well-planned and finely detailed scheme, which reuses existing spaces and creates new ones to produce a modern interchange in the bowels of a major (if not much admired) historic station. All this was achieved in the context of engineering works as difficult as any on the line – one of the civil engineers working at Waterloo described the job as 'the civil engineering equivalent of going to the moon'. Compensation grouting had to be extensively deployed to counter potential
damage to the mainline station and other structures.

When the London & Southampton Railway (subsequently absorbed into the London & South Western) opened in 1838, it terminated at Nine Elms, on the site of the present New Covent Garden Market. Ten years later, the line into Waterloo, carried on a long brick viaduct, was opened. The new station was elevated above street level on a series of brick vaults, retained and extended when the station was comprehensively rebuilt between 1900 and 1922 – with the pompous Victory Arch as its most conspicuous feature. (The undercroft provided an awesome approach to the Waterloo & City – 'the Drain' – opened in 1898.) Nicholas

Grimshaw's International Terminal involved a complete reconstruction of the undercroft level to create a passenger terminal. The JLE has been, in contrast, conservationist.

Initial designs (of 1989) for the JLE station, included in the parliamentary bill, provided for a ticket hall directly underneath the mainline concourse, relatively close to the existing Bakerloo/Northern ticket hall (itself constructed in 1927 after the completion of the Northern Line link between Charing Cross and Kennington). The Underground's presence at Waterloo would have been, as before, completely subsumed within the sprawling mass of the station complex. But there were complications attached to this strategy. No interruption to mainline services could be considered, though major disruption to the passenger concourse was inevitable. Working conditions would be difficult and costs high. The resulting space, though generous in scale, would be entirely subterranean, artificially lit and connected to the street by a passageway. At the last minute JLE's Waterloo team, as youthful and innovative as any on the line, reappraised the project. One of its number, Andreas Gyarfas, waiting for a bus on a wet day, found himself in the 'colonnade' on Waterloo Road (across the road from the Old Vic), a lofty covered area originally used for goods deliveries but latterly turned into an *ad hoc* bus station. It was large and very stoutly constructed, with brick arched vaults on a steel frame supporting the station approach road above, but seemed to be wasted as a bus pull-in. The potential of this space as an alternative location for the ticket hall was subsequently explored during 1991 – the cost savings were considerable, but the practical advantages were even more marked. Integration of bus services has been an important feature of the JLE and an alternative, and very convenient, bus station site (on Tenison Way, linked by escalators to the mainline terminus) had to be identified.

The 'colonnade' now forms the ticket hall and street gateway to the JLE at Waterloo. The aim was to colonize the space, but to restrict structural alterations to the absolute minimum, allowing the integrity of the structure to dominate. 'Outside' has been transformed into 'inside' by inserting frameless structural glazing – engineered to withstand movement in the jack arched roof – behind the existing arches, permitting views, unusual on the Underground system, into the space from the street. Access is at pavement level, with no steps down. The location of the new ticket hall is highly significant, giving both the Underground and Waterloo Station generally a street presence. Inside, the structure has been left relatively unadorned, though some acoustic cladding was necessary to secure the required safety standards. Lighting has been contrived to uplight (and highlight) the historic structure – all electrical services are contained within a utilitarian metal framework for easy maintenance and possible upgrading. Escalators up to the main concourse level are slotted between existing brick arches. To secure adequate circulation space and easy access to the down escalators, a section of brick arches had to be demolished and replaced by a waffle slab constructed in fair faced concrete and supported on big concrete buttresses. The axial flow of the arched roof dictates the planning of the ticket hall, which has a natural flow to the escalators. The latter had to be threaded through the piers and foundations of the brick arches, a complex operation demanding the complete reconstruction of the supporting structure – it is a measure

of the project's success that the maximum settlement recorded is just 26mm (1 inch).

Below ground level, the station is contained within a series of tunnels. The escalators leading down from the ticket hall (two in each tunnel) arrive at an intermediate landing, where the downward route turns at 90 degrees towards another set of escalators giving access to the platform level. One of the drawbacks of relocating the JLE ticket hall is that it is distant from the Bakerloo and Northern line platforms (the existing ticket hall serving these lines has been retained in use). A travellator link, 140 metres (460 feet) long, eases the lot of interchange passengers and also offers a remarkable spatial experience, a transportation version of the Elizabethan long gallery.

The JLE platform layout is conventional in form, with a central concourse between the running tunnels. When the use of the NATM system was being considered (see page 202), there were ideas of combining the concourse and one of the running tunnels in one great space, with knock-on benefits for the engineering of the station. But this strategy was later abandoned. A great deal of attention was given to providing durable finishes within the tunnels. At London Bridge, enamelled cast-iron panels were used. At Waterloo, vacuum-formed aluminium panels were substituted, set within the cast iron tunnel segments. They are lightweight, relatively cheap, and easily replaceable if damaged – the aim was to infill the structure rather than to add another superfluous layer on top of it, so reducing the space. Platform fittings are those common to the line.

'No contrivance – clarity is all' is Roland Paoletti's encapsulation of Waterloo and the other tunnel stations. It was achieved with

remarkably little inconvenience to passengers using the existing Underground and mainline stations. By a sleight of hand, as it were, Waterloo has been transformed and the long-desired Docklands link finally provided.

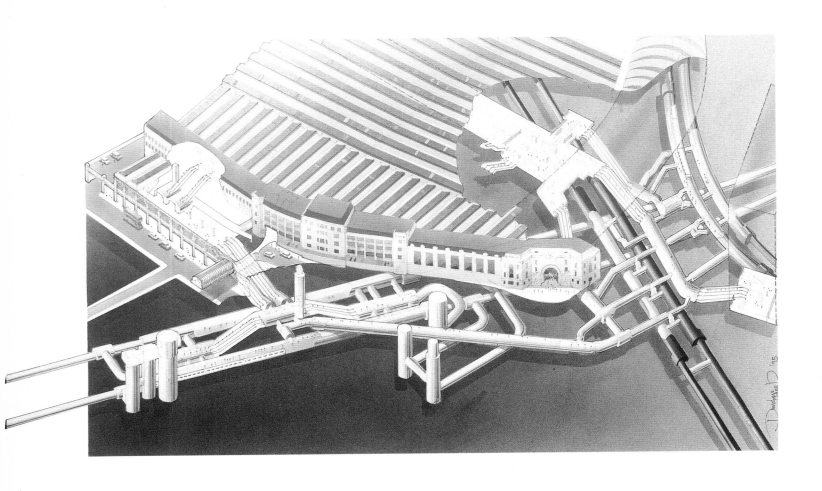

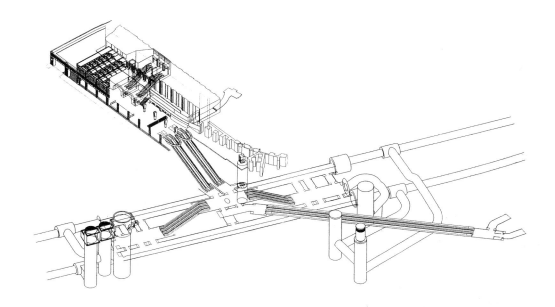

opposite and right
At Waterloo, the new line had to thread its way through a web of existing Underground lines and other obstacles beneath the mainline terminus, which is elevated above street level. Providing clear and direct connections was a key objective of the design process.

below
In 1848 the South-Western Railway extended its line to Waterloo, an event celebrated with this scene in the *Illustrated London News*. Some of the original Victorian brickwork has been retained in the JLE station.

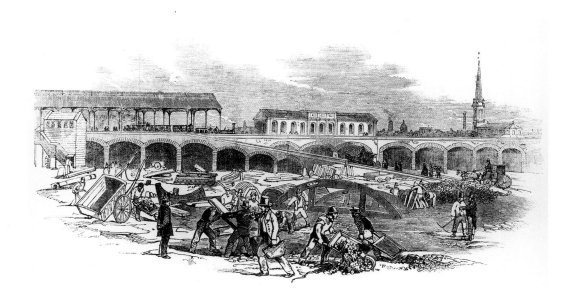

By locating the ticket hall at street level in an undercroft formerly used as a bus station, the JLE architects avoided a major intervention below the mainline station and provided a convenient point of entry.

overleaf
Restored Victorian brickwork and girders contrast with new elements in the ticket hall at Waterloo.

The escalator shafts form a dynamic intervention into the restored undercroft – natural light floods down the escalators.

overleaf left
A 140 metre- (460 foot-) long moving walkway link makes light of the necessarily extended interchange between lines at Waterloo.

overleaf right
The subterranean spaces at Waterloo are entirely architectural, in terms both of space and fit-out.

The glazed platform-edge door screens are an innovation to London, though they are familiar from metro stations in other parts of the world.

southwark

Richard MacCormac of MacCormac Jamieson Prichard (MJP) came to the JLE project with a preconception that: 'The engineers design a system, then the architects dress it up. It was just a matter of deciding which tiles to put on the platform walls.' When it came to subterranean stations, this was all that Holden had been allowed to do as his remit had been to design the ticket halls. But MacCormac soon discovered that the JLE brief was altogether more creative, and more challenging, than mere decoration. In the only JLE station that consciously evokes and makes reference to historical precedents from before the age of the Underground, MJP has created a powerful new architectural image that counterpoises function and artifice, engineering and art.

Southwark Station was an apt commission for an architect who has a strong historical sense and a very broad interest in the visual arts and in their integration into buildings. It is the station serving the new Tate Modern at Bankside, as well as local office workers and a growing residential population – not to forget the Old and New Vic and the Globe theatres. Equally significant is its connection to mainline rail services at Waterloo East (this was probably the factor that swung the decision in favour of building the station when the necessity for it was questioned at planning stage). It was the need to connect with Waterloo East, a bleak outlier of the nearby terminus, which dictated the location at the corner of The Cut and Blackfriars Road, where the station sits among shops, like Underground stations of an earlier age. There could be no single great statement, in the manner of Canary Wharf, say, at Southwark; the genius emerges below ground. MacCormac's achievement was to turn a complex route through the station into an event that could even be enjoyed.

The surface ticket hall is externally quite modest, with clearly Holdenesque touches in its development of an essentially historicist language, but this is seen as merely the base for a future commercial development that will sit on top. The line between Waterloo and London Bridge runs directly underneath the mainline viaduct, so avoiding the piles of recent buildings. To make the station, a central lower-level concourse had to be excavated in addition to the running tunnels – a complex programme of underpinning and grouting was needed to ensure the stability of the Victorian brick arches above. Spaces also had to be found for escape and vent shafts and for the three escalators, which had to be fed between the foundations of the viaduct piers. An abrupt change in direction was then needed to access the ticket hall and street, via another escalator bank. This was accommodated by means of an intermediate concourse, which is also part of the route to and from Waterloo East for interchange passengers.

This concourse provides the centrepiece of the station, a classic instance of a functional space transformed into architecture. MJP is consciously not part of the high-tech tradition from which most of the JLE's architectural consultants stem: engineering in MacCormac's work is usually implicit rather than boldly expressed. Yet the architects' role at Southwark was anything but cosmetic. Nothing on the JLE is superfluous: architecture and engineering form a unity, and at Southwark, architecture helps to mitigate the necessary complexity of the station and make it clear and legible. MacCormac compares the passenger's experience of Southwark to 'an episodic journey', a voyage through a condensed and relatively short-span landscape. The passenger enters the rather low drum of the ticket hall from the street, perhaps reassured by the resonances of Holden and the 1930s, although the materials – white concrete and stainless steel – are entirely contemporary in feel. Descending a few steps from the street is like entering a cave – there is none of the quest for lightness found in other stations on the line – though there is daylight to be seen through the central lantern. The escalators lead down to a very different space, the intermediate concourse, which opens out to a height of 16 metres (52 feet). This space is clearly subterranean, yet it is generously daylit. A monumental concrete screen wall, erected in masonry cast in blocks with lots of sparkle in the mix, set in courses and beautifully finished, contains the great 'scoops' of the escalators. The wall is then balanced with a swooping blue glass curved wall, flooded with daylight from the ticket hall above. The 40 metre- (131 feet-) long glass wall is the result of a collaboration with the artist Alexander Beleschenko and structural engineer Tony Hunt. It contains 660 specially cut pieces of glass, the whole structure based on a segment of a cone and supported on a steel lattice by means of cast steel 'spider' fixings, themselves specially designed to cope with the variations of the layout.

MacCormac explains that the idea of this space, which is both lightweight and monumental, came to him after studying Karl Friedrich Schinkel's illustration of a set for the Queen of the Night's castle in *The Magic Flute*. 'I tend to make unlikely connections', he says. (Even before its completion, this space became a much-publicized image of the JLE and in its unfinished state it was used by English Heritage as the venue for its annual report launch – confirming the station's status as part of 'the heritage of the future'.) MacCormac's first

instinct was to leave the raw concrete of the structure exposed, underlining the paradox of its 'daylit cavern' form, but he moved towards a more finished appearance, recognizing the element of artifice involved and celebrating the chameleon-like versatility of concrete, seen in its boldest structural form in the great roof beams.

MacCormac sees the intermediate concourse as a necessary prelude to the compression of the shafts – another reference to Holden's stations, but a structural device rather than an aesthetic one – which lead down to the lower concourse and platforms. (There were ideas of using mirrors to reflect light down the escalators, but the narrowness of the shafts made this impractical.) The lower concourse is simply a big tunnel on two levels, clad in stainless steel, deliberately left unpolished – 'another Schinkelesque move', says the architect. The staircase joining the levels is illuminated by a boldly modelled 'beacon'. The JLE's stress on uniformity of platform treatments throughout the line ruled out special effects, but the high-quality masonry finish and built-in bench provide a distinctive character. The connection to Waterloo East posed design problems of its own. A new ticket hall had to be contrived underneath the viaduct, but to create an adequate space, the new concourse extends outwards by means of a steel and glass shell – canopy becoming building – which 'wraps' the viaduct. As at London Bridge, Stratford and elsewhere, the JLE has stimulated significant improvements to other transport facilities – MJP's work on the Underground station and link led to a commission to add new canopies and staircases at Waterloo East. The connecting tunnel to Waterloo East had to cope with yet more foundation problems as some of the existing beddings of the brick arches had to be replaced with new portals. The

architecture of the Waterloo East additions is lightweight and glassy, declining to compromise the dignity of the Victorian engineering.

MacCormac's approach at Southwark might have seemed perverse were it not for the success of the completed station. He talks of the station in terms of John Soane, Alvar Aalto and Schinkel as much as Holden. He sees a journey on the Underground as a cultural experience, just like a visit to the Soane Museum. He could have ended up an odd man out. Yet, in its way, Southwark is a paean to the achievements of the engineers and a reflection of the way architects can mould and transform functional space. It will be seen not as an oddity but as one of the most imaginative and enjoyable buildings commissioned by the JLE.

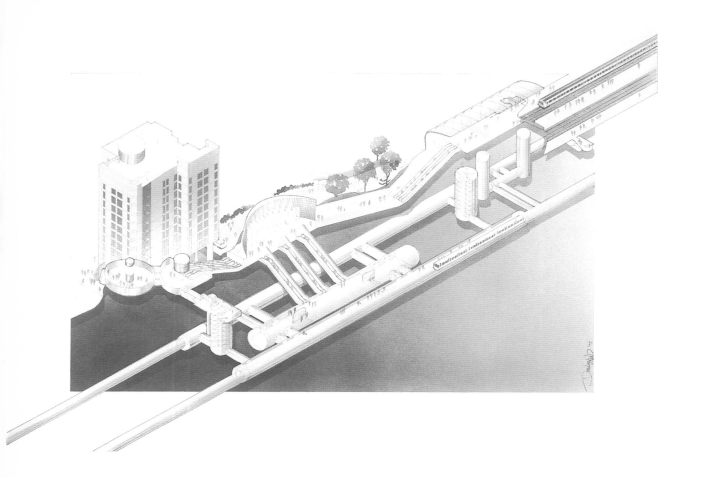

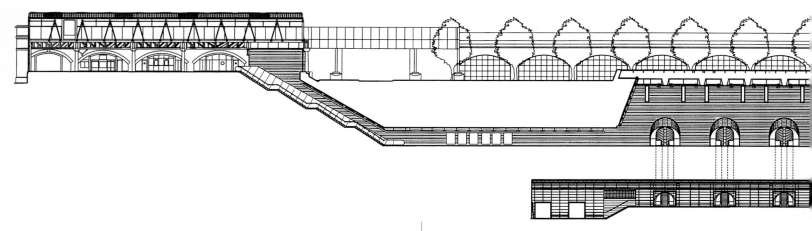

right
Southwark Bankside, with the original Globe Theatre, as it appeared in the 1640s. The rebuilt Globe is one of several cultural centres served by the new JLE station.

opposite and below
Southwark Station had a dual function: providing a gateway to the regenerated Bankside area and a valuable connection between the JLE and the mainline Waterloo East station serving South-east London and Kent. The booking hall is intended as the base of a new commercial development.

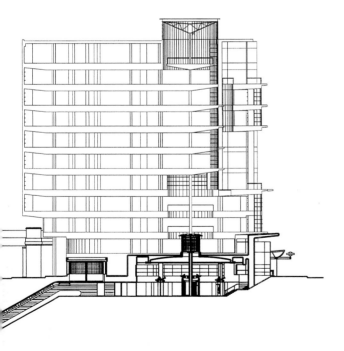

left
The new station has a recognizable, elegant, but undemonstrative, street presence.

opposite
A new wraparound glazed structure provides access from the JLE to the Waterloo East platforms.

overleaf
The ticket hall, with an elegant control box and a glazed rotunda over the escalator shaft, could be seen as an homage to Holden but is part of a progression of spaces which owes rather more to MacCormac's reverence for Soane.

Southwark's monumental intermediate concourse is generously daylit and features a wall of glass which is a fusion of architecture, art and engineering, a theme which pervades the entire station.

overleaf
Inspired by John Soane and the progressive Classical tradition, Richard MacCormac created intensely architectural underground spaces where solid masonry contrasts with the lightness of engineering and the whole is given a special magic by the use of colour.

At platform level, another concourse completes the remarkable spatial odyssey of Southwark.

london bridge

London Bridge was the terminus of London's first railway line, opened in 1836 to Deptford and soon extended to Greenwich. For such a historic location, the present mainline station has little public presence and only sporadic interest internally. The confusing divide between the through ('Kent') platforms formerly used by the South East & Chatham Railway and the terminal area built by the London, Brighton & South Coast Railway has survived half-hearted attempts at improvement. 'One could scarcely believe the misery its lack of accommodation, its narrow platforms and steep, heart-testing steps have caused millions of Londoners over the last hundred years', wrote John Betjeman in *London's Historic Railway Stations* of 1972 – and he was an aficionado of Victorian stations.

The elevation of the station above street level, on a vast area of vaults, made access difficult and blighted the surrounding area, 'indisputably the most hideous of all the termini in external appearance', wrote Alan Jackson of London Bridge. Plans for total reconstruction, Euston-style, were published in the 1960s, but were only partially realized. London Bridge has long been a major commuter station serving the City. The vital tube link arrived there in 1900, after the original route of the City & South London Railway (C&SLR) – which bypassed London Bridge through a 3 metre- (10 feet-) diameter tunnel which still exists and is famous as the scene of Henry Moore's wartime shelter drawings – was superseded by the present Northern Line routing. The surface building of the original C&SLR station survives, at the bottom of the station approach road on Borough High Street – it was served by lifts and was closed in the 1960s. In recent years the Underground station (largely reconstructed in the 1960s) has been remarkable only for its inadequacy and its tortuous connections, in the London Bridge tradition, to the street and mainline platforms.

Routing the JLE through London Bridge to provide a fast link to the West End via Waterloo and the Docklands was always one of the most important benefits of the line, though it posed massive engineering problems. The JLE has also assumed an important role in the regeneration of Southwark – always a poor neighbour to the City but set to become a major tourist destination with the opening of Tate Modern at Bankside. With Southwark Cathedral, the George Inn and other survivals, Borough High Street is a link to Chaucer's London.

The JLE station is one of the biggest on the line, but you look in vain for any external expression of its grandeur, beyond the self-effacing new entrance on the High Street and the sculptural vent shafts designed by architects Weston Williamson (Weston Williamson were also the architects for the station fit-out). But this is not the point. At London Bridge, the JLE has discovered and colonized, as well as created, huge spaces and a new public domain beneath the streets and railway arches. The strategy was developed during 1990 by Roland Paoletti's own team, under the leadership of Martin Short, with Simon Moore working on the platform levels.

The route of the JLE through London Bridge was dictated by the existence of two large, banal 1960s office blocks which flanked the station – to avoid their piling, the line had to pass between them on an east–west route. The contract included a major reconstruction of the Northern Line platforms, including a new concourse area between the platforms. This meant constructing a new section of southbound tunnel under the river, roughly on the line of the old London Bridge, to eliminate the cramped, potentially dangerous conditions that had prevailed there for many decades. With the location of the platforms broadly established, JLE's architects looked at the options for the new concourse, which needed to be far bigger than the existing ticket hall located under the bus station and formed out of the old southbound tunnel. As the new concourse grew, it reached Joiner Street, one of several thoroughfares that passed under the brick arches on which the mainline station was built. It was a dark and dirty chasm, a rat-run for taxis and too intimidating to walk through. But there had once been a service route beneath the station at this level, crossing Joiner Street – indeed, in the very early days of the station, there had been a booking office in Joiner Street, connected to the platforms by separate stairs for first- and second-class passengers. The idea emerged of closing Joiner Street and using it as the link between the Underground and the mainline station, owned at the time by British Rail but subsequently passed to Railtrack. 'It was possibly the most important move on the whole line', says Roland Paoletti, though British Rail and Southwark Council had to be convinced. British Rail, in particular, was concerned about the loss of retail space and slow to grasp the advantages of the strategy.

Today, it is hard to believe that Joiner Street ever carried traffic. It has been redeemed from years of grime, cleaned, lit and animated, a triumph of beneficial reuse. From the Underground ticket hall, passengers can pass across the recast, newly paved street and up escalators to the Kent Line. Via a long-abandoned, but now reopened, route through the vaults to the east, they can access escalators or a lift up to the terminal platforms, using, ironically, a route used by passengers 160 years ago. Behind these lofty new public spaces, huge areas of brick vaults, largely

packed with wine and spirits, remain, maybe one day to be opened up as shopping and eating places. (The London Dungeon, a popular tourist draw, has already colonized some of the area.) Already, people move easily and safely below the station instead of dodging buses and cabs at street level, enjoying long-hidden views of a great historic structure as they do so. The face of London Bridge Station may not be handsome but its guts are certainly impressive. The attention given to the details – the treatment of the cleaned and repaired stone and brick, and the lighting and signage – has paid off.

From the new ticket hall, vastly improved access is provided to the Northern Line by means of a new bank of escalators threaded between great Victorian buttresses. The extremely direct route to the JLE is down a bank of escalators with dramatic turns at an intermediate level – the cast-iron cladding used throughout this station is shown to spectacular effect here, with the roof form evoking the look of Gothic fan vaulting. The escalators disgorge into a tall vaulted space between the JLE platforms. A second escalator bank leads directly to the new Borough High Street entrance, which is also linked to the Northern Line. A convenient link between JLE and Northern Lines was achieved by means of a stair through the JLE concourse roof leading up to the Northern Line interchange passage above. This involved making a 90 degree junction between two sections of tunnel, a complex strategy more often used for narrow ventilating shafts, but an enormous gain in terms of passenger amenity – the double-ended JLE concourse now has clear connections to both main exits (mainline station and Borough High Street) and to the Northern Line and there is little scope for confusion. All of this represents a massive technical achievement.

In technical terms, no site on the JLE was more complicated than London Bridge – tunnelling below the Victorian station and through tracks, Southwark Cathedral and other historic buildings, coping with sewers, services, roads and existing Underground tracks – and at a time (1994) when the Heathrow tunnel collapse caused a reassessment of the techniques used. All this was a major test for the teams of the JLE and the technical contractor Mott MacDonald. Compensation grouting was extensively used to protect streets and buildings in the vicinity. It is the excavation done for the tunnels and concourse of the JLE which is the most impressive tunnelling achievement – a great cavern, particularly imposing before it was lined out, was formed.

The partnership of Andrew Weston and Chris Williamson was the smallest of the practices brought in to work on the JLE stations. Weston Williamson's task was to develop an appropriate language for the fitout of the station, which, though far more accessible than it was, is large and complex. A key design issue, according to Chris Williamson, was 'welding together a very diverse place'. In recent decades, the Underground has concentrated on adding finishes to achieve a 'look', but the ethos of JLE discouraged superfluous finishes. The basic lining of the tunnels at London Bridge was cast iron, in the great Underground tradition. Instructed to cover it up, the architects proposed to develop a system of enamelled cast-iron panels which would complement the basic structure with an incredibly durable system that offered a satisfying return to integrity in place of surface gloss. The inspiration was the classic (and equally indestructible) Aga cooker, admits Williamson. 'Reflecting the strength of the engineering' was the basic theme taken up by the architects and there was a deliberate move to

expose and celebrate structural elements such as the steel opening frames of the central concourse tunnel (11.6 metres/38 feet in diameter).

As everywhere on the JLE, the spaces at London Bridge provide a dramatic contrast to those found elsewhere on the Underground and, indeed, to those that existed here before the reconstruction. The London Bridge project is one of the most important elements in the whole JLE. The rebuilt station serves not only as an interchange with mainline trains, but also as a gateway to 'the Borough', which is becoming a lively area, aware of its past and optimistic about the future. It took the coming of the JLE to achieve significant improvements to the station and its surroundings – all of which were funded by the Underground. Underground London is an alternative face of the capital, often a secret world and sometimes a rather menacing one. The JLE has done much to civilize this. At London Bridge, the JLE has broken down the isolation of the mainline terminal and integrated the world of railways – surface and underground – into the wider life of the city. Not for the first time, the Underground has brought about a profound change in the perception of a whole quarter of London.

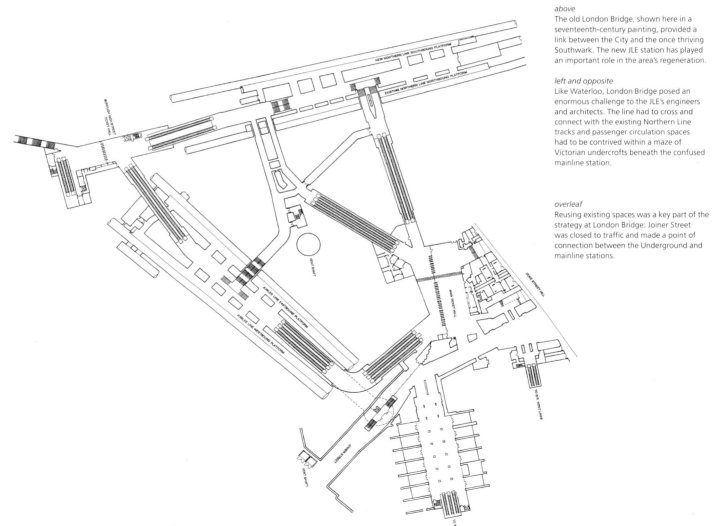

above
The old London Bridge, shown here in a seventeenth-century painting, provided a link between the City and the once thriving Southwark. The new JLE station has played an important role in the area's regeneration.

left and opposite
Like Waterloo, London Bridge posed an enormous challenge to the JLE's engineers and architects. The line had to cross and connect with the existing Northern Line tracks and passenger circulation spaces had to be contrived within a maze of Victorian undercrofts beneath the confused mainline station.

overleaf
Reusing existing spaces was a key part of the strategy at London Bridge: Joiner Street was closed to traffic and made a point of connection between the Underground and mainline stations.

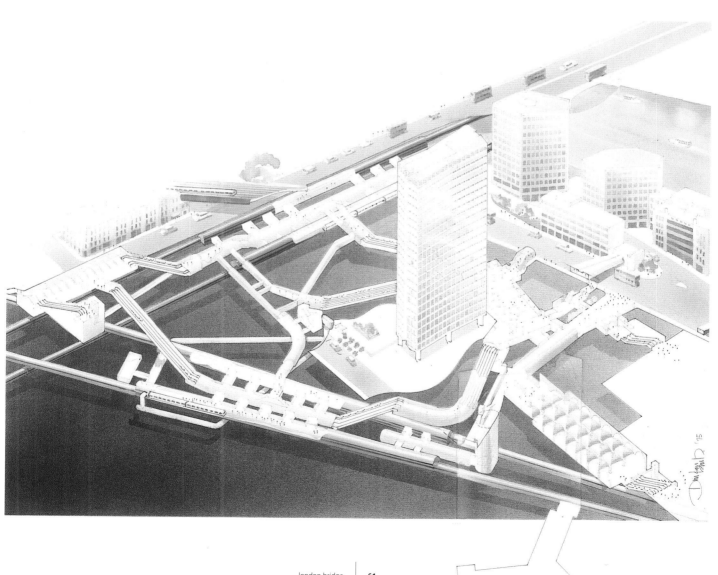

From Joiner Street, a direct escalator link is
now provided to the mainline station.

overleaf
A spacious new ticket hall replaces the
previous cramped facility and serves both
Jubilee and Northern lines.

previous pages
The vast new underground concourse
between the JLE platforms provides a striking
contrast to the restricted conditions prevalent
in older stations on the system.

Enamelled cast-iron panels provide a durable
cladding for the platforms at London Bridge,
and are also a distinctive visual feature.

bermondsey

Westminster Station serves the Houses of Parliament; Canary Wharf is one of the fastest-growing business districts in Europe; and North Greenwich is the gateway to the Millennium Dome. Bermondsey Station is, in contrast, located in an unfashionable quarter of South London, far off the tourist trail. It has been built primarily as a local amenity, a neighbourhood station. Yet it is a decisive architectural statement – a statement about the power of the Underground to regenerate and redefine entire areas of the capital, and a reassertion of Bermondsey's place in the life and culture of London. It also represents the fruits of a positive and creative dialogue between architect, client and engineer.

Ian Ritchie was one of the first architects to be considered by Roland Paoletti and was, says Paoletti, 'structurally minded', an architect who collaborated naturally with structural engineers.

Bermondsey had not always been such a modest place. Its abbey, founded in 1082, dissolved in 1538, and once famous in the Middle Ages for its miracle-working rood, has almost totally vanished. The buildings passed to a Tudor grandee, Sir Thomas Pope, and the house he built on the site survived into the nineteenth century. By the later eighteenth century the area was being subsumed by the growth of London and huge factories, granaries and wharves were developed there, forming an industrial base that only withered after the Second World War. By 1836, Bermondsey was connected to London's first modern transit system, the London & Greenwich Railway (L&GR), carried on a viaduct of 878 arches – still the longest in London – to avoid the waterlogged ground below. Later in the century, one of London's first electric tramways opened along the Jamaica Road, later to be the site for the JLE station.

Jamaica Road is now a teeming traffic artery which frames a distant view of the Canary Wharf tower. The site was overlooked by residential blocks and closely circumscribed by streets, factors that would mould the project. It was anticipated that provision for a development on top of the station would provide some financial return, although passenger numbers were projected at less than 10 per cent of those at Canary Wharf. Russell Black, the JLE civil engineering project director, together with Roland Paoletti, had already produced a construction diagram for the station as part of the parliamentary submission. This diagram consisted of a cut-and-cover box for approximately a third of the station length, the remaining two-thirds being conventional bored tunnels. The box, although marginally more expensive than a London Underground station constructed from an assembly of vertical and inclined shafts for escalators, lifts and plant, was safer and quicker for construction. This was particularly important, given the ground conditions at Bermondsey, the restricted site and close proximity of residential property. The box also offered great intrinsic flexibility.

Like other JLE architects, Ritchie was not familiar with the ethos of civil engineering. Establishing a working dialogue with the engineers, Sir William Halcrow, was vital. To achieve this, the architects had to understand the techniques of civil engineering below ground: essentially it is about responding to geological conditions with an appropriate construction technique in order to provide the permanent envelope of the station. This enabled the architects to design with the engineers using a shared understanding of construction.

There were, however, other important issues to be considered. The King's Cross Station fire of 1987 had reinforced the case for stations where public routes were made very clear – an open, day-lit space is more legible than the tight tunnels found elsewhere on the system. There were also issues of personal security in a relatively little-used, lightly staffed station in an inner-city area. The idea of transparency was to be pursued in the design of the surface building, which London Underground wanted to be highly durable, and equally, a visible contribution to the regeneration of the area. These ideas had to be integrated with, and balanced against, basic engineering priorities.

A concise design philosophy emerged, comprising three key principles. Firstly, to bring a perceptible sensitivity and designed ambience to the public, through the use of natural light and clear spatial experiences. Secondly, to manipulate these elements so they respond positively to the demands of security, durability and safety, bringing about the integration of structure, servicing, architectural layout and design. And thirdly, to expose the civil engineering structure of the station box and platform tunnels in order to express the primary elements of construction and to provide a clarity of material expression for all other components within the station.

The tunnels in this section of the Line skim the dense waterbearing Thanet Beds, pressurized by an aquifer. (The presence of pressurized ground water produced the short-lived Bermondsey Spa, opened in 1770 only 500 metres/a third of a mile from the present station site.) This is the first major construction project for London Underground within this ground strata, and has only been made possible due to recent advances made in tunnel boring machine technology using an earth-pressure balanced tunnel boring machine. This machine, unlike open-face tunnelling, relies on forming seals between the excavated material and the work area to exclude unstable ground and water from the construction activities. The diaphragm walls that form the station box are constructed in similar conditions and resist the massive combined forces of ground and water pressures. A fusion of architecture and engineering was developed. To obtain the requisite legibility and transparency, the basic idea of the box was transformed by three strategic moves. Firstly, by adjusting the box profile and track centres, it was possible to reorganize the station to provide a combination of deep horizontal open trusses and flat slabs to act as the bracing to the diaphragm walls, with the vertical load of the trusses supported by the diaphragm walls and assisted by free-standing columns. The second move was the introduction of four continuous blade walls that define zones for vertical circulation platforms and ventilation equipment. The blade walls stiffen the horizontal base slab against upward hydrostatic pressure and create a void in the centre of the box between platform level and ground level for the escalators. Thirdly, the introduction of the void between the blade walls resulted in the elimination of all temporary works in connection with the diaphragm walls and enabled the station to be constructed top-down. This resolved the all-important means of construction. The diaphragm walls were installed from the surface forming the outer enclosure to the box, the trusses bracing them being cast on the ground starting at the level closest to the surface, with subsequent trusses being cast after removal of spoil. The planning of the station played an important role in the building process, maximizing freedom for vertical construction movement.

Bermondsey Station reflects a process of questioning and rethinking by challenging the traditional ways of operating. Its pragmatism, rooted in ideals, epitomizes the thinking behind the JLE and explains why the line is a turning-point for London Underground and for London. Ian Ritchie recalls that his first instinct was to seek to create a station like Earl's Court or Farringdon, with day-lit platforms, but the engineering constraints – the deep-bored tunnels had to be integrated into the tightly constrained station box – ruled this out. The practicalities of the situation had to be accepted, and Bermondsey is not set in a shallow open trench. The architects' central objective – clarity within a naturally lit space – was, however, achieved. The interior of the station is dramatic without being intimidating.

Externally, this principle of clarity is clearly expressed. Instead of giving the building a solid, defensive look, the station is entered through a glazed pavilion, its elegance an expression of the way in which the JLE is transforming London. There are views from the street into the booking hall and escalator box. The roof, clad in translucent glazing (which runs on a grid from east to west, echoing the flow of the building from the tracks up), sweeps up towards Jamaica Road to become a highlight on this drab thoroughfare. A continuous illuminated blue glass frieze and bench provide a visual link from street to platform – the 'jewellery' of the station. These devices, together with carefully designed platform equipment, signage and services in the public areas, provide the transition between the scale of civil engineering and human proportions. There is delicacy as well as durability about this station and it respects the area in which it stands without condescension. For Ritchie, this was 'our most complex job so far'. By confronting the issues of engineering and transport design, rather than attempting to put a gloss on them, Ian Ritchie Architects, together with the civil engineers and the diligent attention of Paoletti's site team, has created, within a confined site, an exceptional public building for twenty-first-century London.

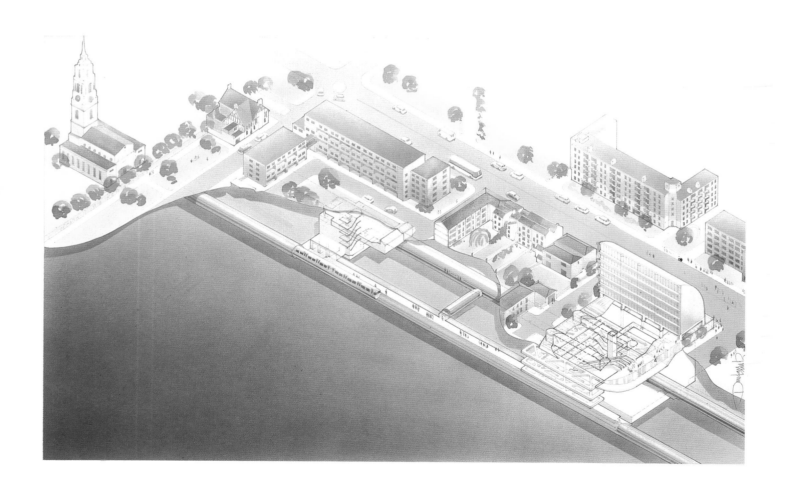

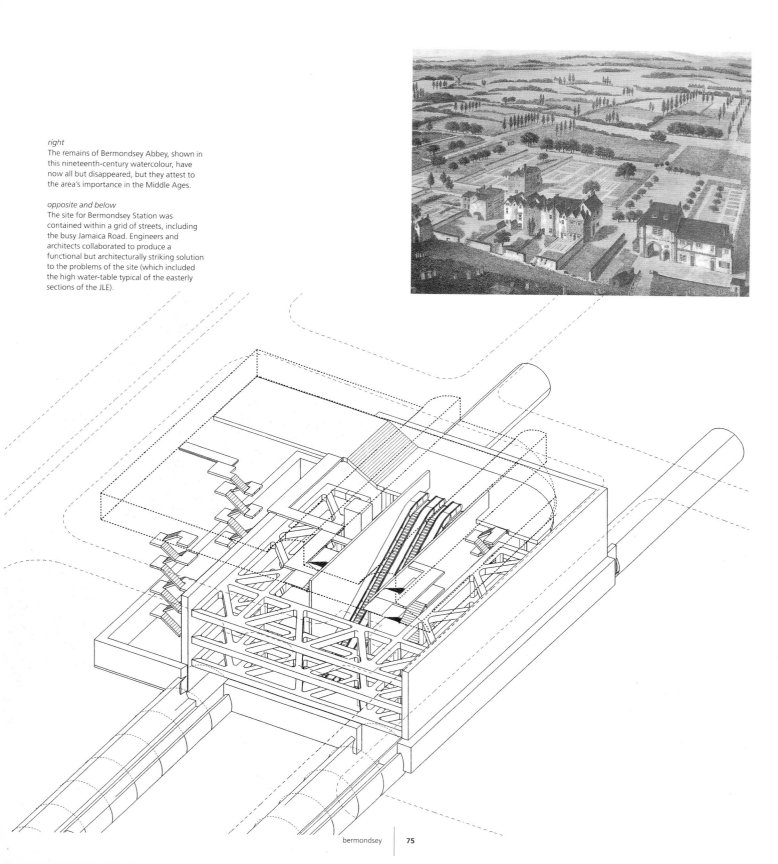

right

The remains of Bermondsey Abbey, shown in this nineteenth-century watercolour, have now all but disappeared, but they attest to the area's importance in the Middle Ages.

opposite and below

The site for Bermondsey Station was contained within a grid of streets, including the busy Jamaica Road. Engineers and architects collaborated to produce a functional but architecturally striking solution to the problems of the site (which included the high water-table typical of the easterly sections of the JLE).

At street level, the station provides a welcoming refuge from heavy traffic – there is no attempt at a defensive look despite the harsh location.

The escalator box is at right angles to the main entrance on Jamaica Road – a practical necessity, but adding to the experience of using the building.

The blue glass platform seat at Bermondsey is a unique feature and was seen by Ian Ritchie as part of the 'jewellery' of the station.

At Bermondsey, natural light fills the escalator box and filters down to platform level.

canada water

The Surrey Docks area, and much of South-East London, has been poorly served by public transport in the past, but the interchange at Canada Water – incorporating a JLE station and a bus station – now brings the West End and Docklands within easier reach of travellers from Deptford, Peckham and beyond. The Underground station, designed as the JLE pilot scheme, is of interest both for the way it encapsulates ideas that were central to the entire design process and for the way in which it differs from its neighbouring stations. For John Self, London Underground general manager for the Jubilee and East London Lines, Canada Water Station (where these lines intersect) is the 'pivot of the whole line', a role that is signified by the dramatic glazed drum, 25 metres (80 feet) across, a landmark in the Surrey Docks area and a vertical counter-point to the essentially horizontal, subterranean splendours of Canary Wharf and North Greenwich.

The station is a much needed and widely supported landmark for the area. There were never great runs of warehouses in the Surrey Commercial Docks – the principal trade was in timber – and most of the docks themselves have been filled and replaced by a drab landscape of low-rise, neo-vernacular housing, retail and 'leisure' sheds, and the huge, blank, automated printing plants which are the manufacturing arm of the newspapers' editorial offices located across the Thames in Canary Wharf. Before the arrival of the JLE the only Underground line to penetrate Docklands was the East London Line (ELL) that runs through the Brunels' pioneering Thames Tunnel and passes under the site at Canada Water on its way to New Cross, but there was no stop here – the station site was part of the former Albion Dock. Providing an interchange with the ELL, previously a backwater of the system (but likely,

early in the twenty-first century, to be extended northwards to Islington and to become a major transport link), was a prime objective of the Canada Water Station project. A further element of continuity is the fact that Canada Water was a projected station location on the original Fleet Line – the only one to be realized on the JLE.

Canada Water was the first JLE station to be designed. The initial sketch was made overnight in the first days of the project team's existence. It was immediately used as the pilot study and then developed by Herron Associates and used to illustrate the project's intent for its stations. Widely circulated and closely scrutinized for economy, the plans were quickly approved and frozen. Apart from a revised design for the drum and economies made during construction, it is remarkable how little the station has changed since then: it retains much of the character of a sketch.

Paoletti compares the station to an abstract and recounts how Fernand Léger described one of his canvases as 'a battle of volumes brutally overlapping one another, bathed in a cool light. They are made up of ordinary people seen among ordinary objects made extraordinary by their juxtaposition in space'. Likewise, he says the design of Canada Water is flexible, anti-dogmatic and very simple and has to do with moving people over, under, around and through the architectural object. Both in its overall concept and in its parts, economy and a simplicity of construction have been the controlling factors. Canada Water is the extension's most thrifty station and the one most dependent on movement and people for its effect.

The design of the drum, characterized by its own economy and simplicity, was developed with engineers Buro Happold. Initial ideas of protecting the glass with a screen of perforated metal were later dropped with the introduction of the bus station, but account for the oversailing roof, which coincidentally recalls Holden's Arnos Grove, though that station has little in common with the bold engineering statement of Canada Water. The drum is more than a visual beacon to the district – it creates an interplay between interior and external space, and their activities. It bathes the heart of the station – its primary internal ordering devices, the glazed bridge, the triple-height volume, and the cascade of escalators below it – with ever-changing natural light.

The basic diagram of Canada Water Station, as drawn up in 1990 and developed with engineers Robert Benaim & Associates, is in fact a modified version of a typical Hong Kong interchange station: a large box, 22 metres (72 feet) deep, constructed in the cut-and-cover method, with internal spaces formed on a short-span, multi-column system and connected by banks of escalators. There are three levels: ticket hall, ELL platforms and JLE, the two lines crossing each other diagonally. For Paoletti, Canada Water is a conventional civil engineer's solution, transformed by the introduction of the lantern and the consequent play on the spaces below.

Although Canada Water is a tough, matter-of-fact station, the planning and structural issues were by no means straightforward. Integrating the ELL greatly complicated the task of constructing the station box (though the fact that the ELL was eventually closed for over a year helped), while the close proximity of high-rise housing provided another constraint. The decision to construct a bus station as part of the Canada Water Interchange was taken while the project was underway, though it had always been envisaged that, as at Southwark and Bermondsey, the site above the station would be

commercially developed after the opening of the JLE; the station's massive columns provide foundations for the development of a multi-storey commercial building. There are three separate entrances to the station. Two are from Surrey Quays Road, housed in beautifully detailed glazed pavilions, and lead to a bridge which spans the great space within the drum. The third entrance leads from the bus station, accessible by a choice of lift or broad staircase. The route down through the station is immediately clear – there are views from the entrance down to the ticket hall and of the escalators leading to the platforms. There is no sense of an overriding architectural concept or *parti* imposed on operational requirements, but rather the impression that architectural statements and functional needs are balanced. The ELL platform spaces are relatively low, like those of other stations on that line. The rationale is practical, but the effect stresses that this is part of the old Underground, whereas the dynamic spaces above express the spirit of the new century. The whole structure is expressed and underpinned, actually and metaphorically, by the great columns that extend right through it.

Finishes in the station have been kept simple. The shuttered concrete is standard in its mix and finish, with none of the special effects demanded by other JLE architects, though blue bands, intended to assist the visually impaired, provide an element of colour. Economical grey mosaic is used extensively.

A highly practical approach equally prevailed for the incorporation of platform services such as lighting, public address and fire control systems. A well-designed metal grid runs throughout the platforms, and a heavy-duty system in the low ticket hall is well able to resist vandalism and, more importantly, to cope with

an ever-changing battery of equipment. (The Underground has experienced immense problems in upgrading the highly finished, often listed stations of the Holden/Pick era.)

Canada Water is already revolutionizing the life of the Surrey Docks area, long considered remote from central London, as rising property prices and a profusion of nearby developments confirm.

'The most expensive solution isn't necessarily the most useful', says Robert Birbeck, a key member of the team. 'This is a station that can cope with the demands of a modern railway system, where things are bound to change.' The station is an intriguing building constrained by an enforced economy. It is unselfconciously utilitarian but nevertheless convincing in its toughness and durability. Designed with the railway operation firmly in mind, it is reportedly one of the most popular stations on the Line for the Underground's own staff: its apparent scorn for artifice does not diminish its spacious, sunny comfort.

Economical, rigorous and beautiful, the bus station, designed by Eva Jiricna Architects, acts as an elegant counterpoint. From an early stage, it was clear that the bus station would need to be substantially enclosed, not only for passenger comfort but to minimize the effects of noise and pollution on the residents of the high-rise residential blocks that closely adjoin the site. In contrast to the Foster-designed bus station at North Greenwich, Canada Water provides an overall enclosure where buses wait under cover. Passenger facilities are concentrated along a central spine adjacent to the JLE entrance. The structural support for the roof had to come from this spine, to avoid intrusions into the parking and boarding spaces. The intention was to create an agreeable environment for passengers, to express the new-found

dignity of bus travel and to relate the structure to that of the JLE-station, already under way.

The spine building, which largely houses surface elements of the JLE station, is treated as a solid mass. Over it sails the great roof, which sits on five slender steel columns, spaced 16 metres (52 feet) apart. From the columns, a series of steel rib trusses spring out, braced by steel struts which are tied back to a central truss running the length of the building.

Jiricna is an architect with roots in engineering, a designer who enjoys 'leaning on logic' as she expresses it – avoiding the arbitrary, but pushing rational structure to the point where it becomes highly expressive and, indeed, beautiful. She freely concedes that there is an element of composition in the Canada Water roof, even an attempt to evoke the elegance of natural forms, but the good looks are underwritten by an emphasis on performance and durability. The 100 metre- (33 feet-) long main truss, formed out of six separate sections, site-welded into two pieces and craned into position on the columns, is clad in toughened glass, a brilliant touch that allows the structure to be seen. But there is a reason for the cladding – part of a strategy to deter pigeons. A similar logic underlay the cladding of the roof canopies, hiding the cantilever ribs but denying a foothold to the birds.

The junction between bus and Underground stations was clearly a sensitive point from the start. A swirling, glazed concourse, the glass canopy supported on tapered, pre-cast columns, wraps around the station drum and links to the bus station, protecting travellers from the weather.

Amazingly, the delicacy and bravura of Jiricna's work has translated well into the demanding world of transport, where its essential strength and structural integrity come into their own.

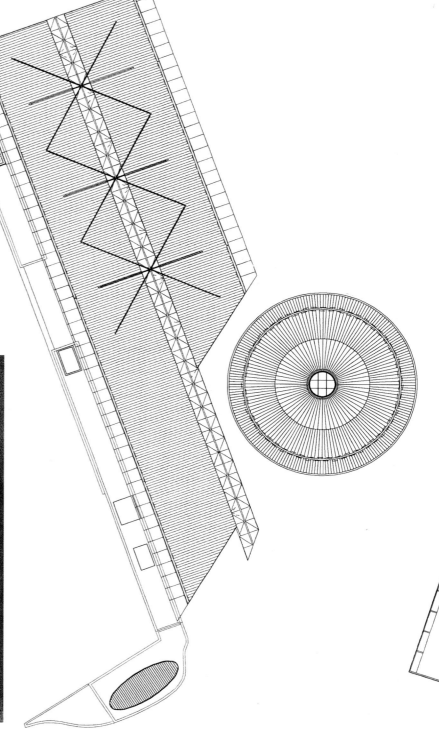

right and opposite
At Canada Water, the JLE crosses the Underground's East London Line, and a new point of interchange is created. The circular station drum forms a counterpoint to the great roof of Eva Jiricna's bus station (the rectangular structure on the left of the plan).

below
The southern entrance to Marc and Isambard Bunel's Thames Tunnel in 1836. The tunnel is now used by the East London line which passes through Canada Water Station.

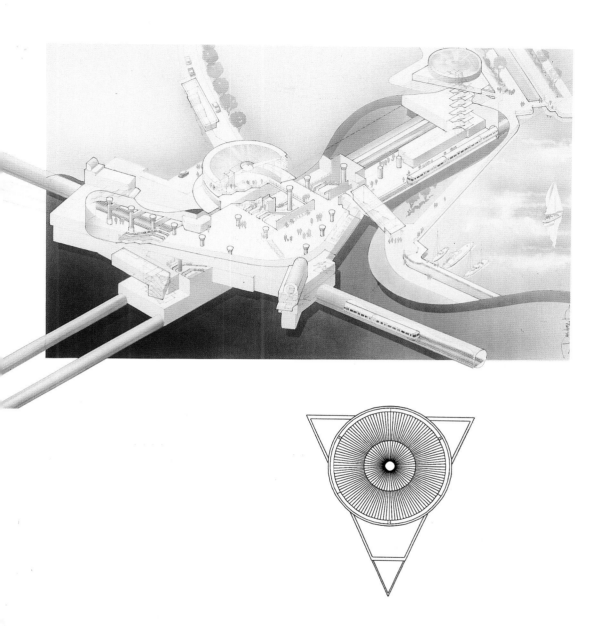

By day a distinctive landmark, at night the station drum glows welcomingly – a point of identity in a still developing post-industrial landscape.

overleaf
The round drum of the Underground station and the linear spine of the bus station are both glazed and transparent. As visitors move through the building they experience a visual interplay of shapes.

The lantern is the heart of the Underground station, a dramatic point of arrival and departure and a symbol of Canada Water's role as the operational pivot of the JLE.

The structure of the station is in ordinary concrete, frankly exposed and unadorned. The columns are designed to carry the commercial development planned to sit on top.

Light filters down from the drum to platform level, through the concrete structure of the station box.

canary wharf

Given the crucial role played by Canary Wharf in the genesis of the JLE (see page 14), it is appropriate that this station is a magnificent and luminous cathedral of underground travel. Canary Wharf is one of the most successful and rapidly expanding business districts in Europe, with a working population (in 1999) of over 25,000 and set to double within the next decade.

London's dock system took over a century, and a vast investment of capital and human effort, to develop. Within 50 years of the completion of the last of the Royal Docks in 1921, the docks were in inexorable decline and by 1981 the last had been closed. The first moves towards 'regeneration' were made in the early 1970s and transport was already seen as the key issue. The docklands area was a closed world: goods, not people, moved in and out of it and its workforce was part of a tight local community. Only one part of the Underground system, the East London Line, penetrated the area – opened in 1869, it made use of Marc Isambard and Isambard Kingdom Brunel's Thames Tunnel. The establishment of the London Docklands Development Corporation (LDDC) by the Thatcher government in 1981 gave a new urgency to the transport issue, though early developments were low-rise and low-density, easily serviced (it seemed) by the relatively cheap Docklands Light Railway system. By 1987, Canary Wharf had a rail link of sorts to the City, via Tower Gateway. The publication that year of grandiose plans for development in the former West India Docks, commissioned initially by G. Ware Travelstead and later progressed by Olympia & York, highlighted the inadequacy of public transport provision for the site.

The selection of Foster & Partners as architect for the Canary Wharf station provided a counterpoint to the predominant look of Canary Wharf's first development phase – a showy, transatlantic post-modern. Roland Paoletti's first instinct was to commission stations from relatively young practices. Foster & Partners was already a world-famous office, but it had to go through the same selection process as any other firm.

Having succeeded in the tender process, Foster & Partners were appointed in 1990. The site had been decided. It would be a cut-and-cover box (its size determined by the need to provide a cross-over point where trains could terminate and return to central London) within an arm of the former dock, south of Canada Square. The reaction against the ruthless infilling of so many historical docks, which were now seen as an amenity, produced a requirement from the LDDC, very difficult to realize, that the dock be left intact and the water reinstated after the completion of construction works. However, this demand was technically unacceptable to the operational railway and the requirement was eventually overcome. As compensation for the loss of water, however, a new public park was planned to sit on top of the station.

The designs for Canary Wharf Station developed quickly – there were just nine months to produce drawings. 'We kept asking ourselves the question: what is the essence of a twenty-first-century tube station?' recalls partner-in-charge David Nelson.

London's Underground system had always been congested – a staggering 9 million people travelled on the Metropolitan Line between Paddington and Farringdon in the first year of its operation in 1863. The Underground was ingeniously slotted into the existing cramped urban pattern – London had had no Baron Haussmann to plan its streets. The consequence was that stations were traditionally relatively small and often complicated in plan, labyrinths set to induce claustrophobia. At Canary Wharf (and North Greenwich) these constraints did not apply. The station design could reflect the current and future needs of the site. The urban form of Canary Wharf was established – large blocks around generous public spaces. But there was much more to come and Nelson recalls the words of Frederick Law Olmsted, creator of New York's Central Park: 'Twenty years hence, the town will have enclosed Central Park. Let us consider therefore what will at that time be satisfactory, for it is then that the design will have to be really judged.' These were prophetic words for Canary Wharf, especially since there was to be a new park over the station. Another Manhattan model might be Grand Central Station, used by huge numbers of people every day, a microcosm of the city as a whole, a meeting place and an urban forum as well as a transportation hub, yet never giving the impression of congestion. The soaring space in the building alleviates any feeling of crowding. The same is true of great historic stations in London such as King's Cross and Paddington.

At Canary Wharf it was predicted that 50,000 or more passengers might pass through the station daily at peak periods. The scale and clarity of circulation in the public areas was therefore critical. It was entirely practical to create generous spaces, given the site and the method of construction. The parameters of the scheme were the location of the tracks, construction constraints and safety requirements such as escape and fire control systems.

A big hole had to be dug for the station. This meant retaining the great volume created by the excavation and using it to form a very clear and intelligible station where passenger routes were instantly apparent, and

that made maximum use of available natural light.

The first stage of the construction process (authorized within days of the government green light to the JLE project) was completed in summer 1994, with the handover of the reclaimed site, once it had been drained and cleared of accumulations of river mud and contained by cofferdams set within the listed dock walls. Diaphragm walls were built within the box and work began excavating down a further 24 metres (78 feet). It was originally intended that the site have developments on both sides, but as a result of the early Nineties recession these plans were not realized and only one side was built on. In order to prevent the sway that would be caused by the resulting lack of construction on one side of the site, deep tension piles were used.

There is a single, very large passenger concourse, nearly 265 metres (869 feet) long, containing two ticket halls divided by glazed screens: this produced one of the most impressive new interiors in London. Nelson and his team wanted to achieve great elegance: the elliptical columns had to be kept slender and were designed for high performance, including being capped by bearings to allow for a degree of movement. The mezzanine concourse level, weighing 2,500 tonnes, was suspended from above, so as to avoid intrusions into the platform space. To respond to these requirements, the box itself was stiffened and the walls thickened at considerable cost. The overall cross-section of the station became a 'hammer head', with the concourse spreading out over the tracks. Essential services were concentrated at one end and the booking offices, staff accommodation and other facilities were placed along each side of the concourse to keep it open and free of intrusions – an arrangement so clear

and simple that it hardly needed conventional signage.

The dramatic use of natural light has been a key feature of Norman Foster's architecture over three decades, so that the architects immediately sympathized with Paoletti's wish to use daylight as far as possible in the JLE stations. For the Bilbao Metro, Foster had used great curved, glazed canopies at street level to bring light underground (these became known locally as 'Fosteritos'). The two main entrance canopies at Canary Wharf are a development of the Fosteritos (one of which is reproduced almost verbatim as a subsidiary western entrance), which glow at night. The canopies scoop up daylight and direct it downwards by refraction. Their design is very complex. Perfected in consultation with engineers Ove Arup & Partners and with as many as 96 distinct curved glass sections, they have more in common with the great roof at Foster's American air museum in Duxford than with the smaller, simpler Bilbao canopies. The fine-quality *in situ* concrete of the roof is designed to reflect light and is in tune with the overall theme of the station.

The architects of Canary Wharf have created a station that looks built to last for centuries, designing in as much as they could (such as lighting and speakers) to minimize the changes that they know will take place. It is, however, much more than a response to a practical brief, though it bears the stamp of the overall philosophy behind the JLE. The loftiness and purity of the interior reflects a typically Fosterian search for perfection. The completed station is a classic example of transport architecture at its best. Foster's achievement has been to meet the requirements of a modern, heavily used transport system while simultaneously making a work of art. Canary Wharf demonstrates what the

future of underground station planning should be. It is the point of reference for new railway architecture in London.

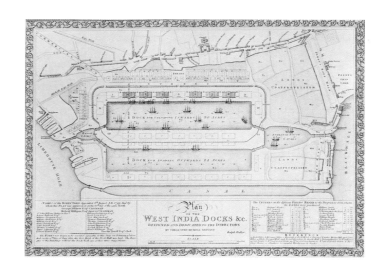

above left
The abandoned West India Docks – shown here when they were a thriving concern in the plan of 1802 – provided the site for the Canary Wharf Development. The JLE station now fills part of the lower basin.

left and opposite
Canary Wharf Station, serving the huge commercial development built on part of the redundant West India Docks, sits within the basin of a former dock.

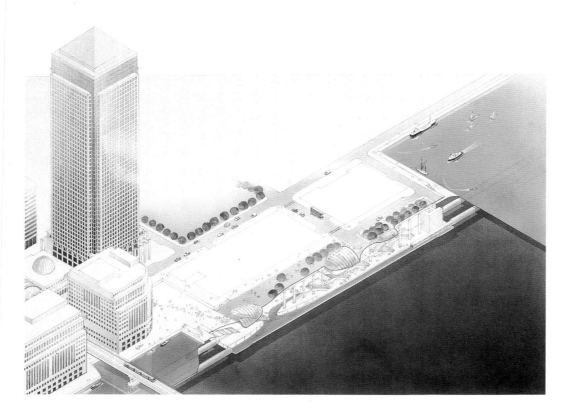

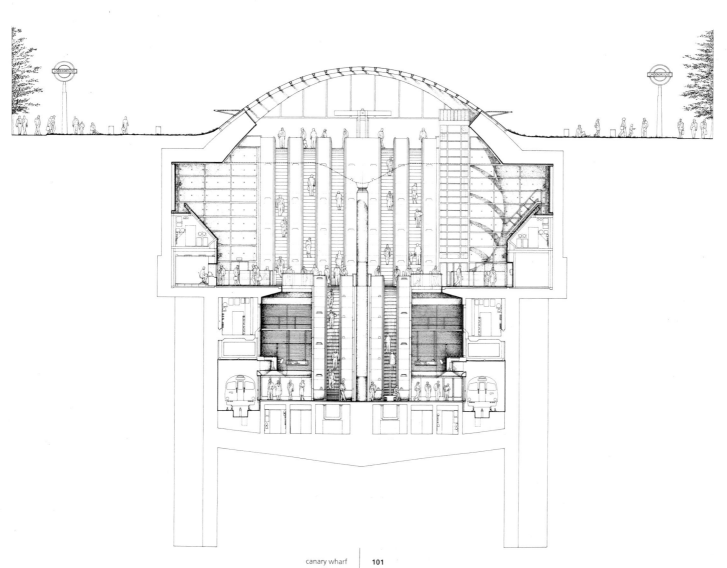

Externally, the station, which sits below a new public park, is distinguished only by its glazed entrance canopies, designed to draw large volumes of commuters into the escalator box.

The glazed canopies over the entrances are a source of natural light – they are remarkable for their sophisticated glazing technology.

opposite
Foster's station is notable for its combination of engineering strength and architectural elegance.

right
The heads of the columns supporting the concourse roof at Canary Wharf contain bearings and are designed to allow a degree of movement within the structure.

Jubilee line

The concourse at Canary Wharf is on the scale of a mainline station or airport terminal, a noble concrete-vaulted space made for large passenger volumes. Lighting is skilfully used to highlight the drama of the space.

left
Ticketing facilities, staff accommodation and other services are neatly contained within linear structures along the edge of the main concourse.

opposite
Even at platform level, there are views upwards to the daylight.

north greenwich

When North Greenwich Station was being planned, there was no indication that it would eventually become one of the most heavily used stations in London – the Millennium Festival and the Dome, which would share the site, were still in the future. The site on the Greenwich peninsula was the most desolate on the JLE, having been entirely occupied for over a century by one of the largest gasworks in Europe, which poured pollution into the soil. After the closure and clearance of the gasworks, a series of proposals were brought forward for the development of the land by British Gas and its subsidiary, Port Greenwich Ltd, the owners of the site. With the future of the latter uncertain, it was at one time planned to abandon the proposed station – or at least to build a basic box to be fitted out at some future date. Only in 1996 did the plans for the Millennium Festival and Dome emerge, but by this time the JLE station was fortunately already well under way – its existence, indeed, made the Dome possible.

Connected to local bus routes, North Greenwich Station offers deepest South-east London a rapid link to the West End and Docklands – up to 75 per cent of regular station users are likely to continue their journeys by bus, though there will also be a 1,000-space car park. (New housing developments will be within walking distance of the station.) A bus station was planned from the beginning as an element of the scheme, but the commission (from London Transport Property) went to Foster & Partners as late as August 1996 – after the future of the area had been clearly mapped out.

The bus station is a huge and beautiful object, with a spreading 160-metre (524-feet) wingspan that draws in the passengers. Built in a year, it demonstrates the Foster office's ability to transform a relatively mundane use into something celebratory and romantic and to re-define an unpromising building type. The form of the great aluminium roof, 6,500 square metres (69,965 square feet) in area, is derived from a section of a hypothetical 1,000 metre- (3,280 feet-) diameter dome. Everything is very lightweight and since the structure, designed in collaboration with engineers Anthony Hunt Associates, could not rest on the escalator hall of the station, it is cantilevered off perimeter column supports incorporated into the glass cladding, with steel 'trees' taking over where clear span spaces were required – at the entrance to the Underground station, where the span is 30 metres (98 feet), and in the drop-off areas. The structure, complex in design but deceptively simple in appearance, has to accommodate possible movement resulting from the station box's location on a heavily waterlogged site. Naturally ventilated and energy efficient, the concourse is fundamentally a very large bus shelter, screened from the fierce winds that sometimes sweep the Greenwich peninsula. It is welcoming, transparent, delicate and sits lightly on its site. By night, a sophisticated lighting scheme, devised by Claude Engle, uses specially designed fittings to provide both up- and down-lighting and effective but dramatic illumination for the public spaces, bouncing light off the great roof.

Having been first approached by Roland Paoletti in 1990, the firm of Alsop Lyall & Störmer – under partner-in-charge John Lyall and working with engineers Robert Benaim & Associates – developed the Underground station to tender stage in 1993. At this point the JLE architectural team carried on the project by providing full construction drawings and completing the design in detail, as was also the case at London Bridge and Canada

Water. The station was seen as the key to regenerating the land, but as Will Alsop recalls, 'its place in the projected development wasn't clear, nor was it given any prominence in the master plan then in force.' The basic idea for the Underground station was that of a two-level cut-and-cover box. There were other Underground stations – South Kensington, for example – that sat in an open cutting. With no immediate prospects for profitable development over the tracks at North Greenwich, it would surely be much cheaper not to build a roof. Fresh air and daylight had their attractions. An open station would be safer and more secure, it was argued. Surrounded by a park or green square in the London tradition, it would have provided a prestigious high-value focus to the area. But the idea, strongly backed by Roland Paoletti and at the highest level by London Underground, foundered on engineers' objections based on the difficulty of dealing with the polluted site, and the station was given a 'lid' with a view to future development on top.

Despite this reverse, the architects were able to capitalize on the benefits offered by the clear site to produce a station impressive not only for its scale but equally for its expressive and dramatic detail and virtuoso use of materials. The site was not only polluted but heavily waterlogged, with ground conditions (a mix of clay and gravel) that produced great difficulties for the tunnellers. A coffer-dam had to be constructed before the huge, 358 metre- (1,174 feet-) long box for the station could be excavated. The excavation of the box opened the way for tunnelling operations to begin in the direction of Canning Town, under the Thames. Construction of the station began in summer 1995. The box is so big because North Greenwich is both a place where trains can reverse as well as the starting point of

the JLE's potential extension into the Royal Docks: this is the only station with three JLE platforms.

The initial idea of the 'open air' scheme, to build a suspended concourse from which passengers would descend to the open platforms, survived in revised form into the (more costly) scheme as built, the concourse becoming a great parabolic 'boat', clad in stainless steel, hanging from the roof on slender steel struts and housing the ticket hall. It also serves as a smoke duct and services spine – indeed, the parabolic shape was seen as the best way to effectively minimize the visual bulk of the duct from the platforms below. It was the absence of a traditional full-width concourse floor that gave the architects the chance to exploit the large internal volume of the station – there are dramatic views down to the platforms from concourse level. Recalls John Lyall: 'It was very important for us that the passengers should "read" and clearly understand the layout of the station, and that they should be uplifted by the space.' The roof itself is supported by 21 pairs of 13 metre- (42 feet-) high columns in 'V' formations. Originally intended to be pre-cast, these were, in fact, constructed in situ and clad in mosaic, a highly practical material used elsewhere on the JLE – according to Robert Benaim, in structural terms 'they are at the limit of the feasible'. The columns stand on a base slab up to 2 metres (6.5 feet) thick, pinned to the clay beneath and designed to counter any tendency for the station to float in the saturated ground.

At North Greenwich, the platforms and trains are integrated into the main volume of the station, providing something of the drama of large mainline stations – the decision to install platform screens in all below-ground stations along the line made this layout acceptable. There is great clarity, a fundamental feature of the

JLE, but also a dynamic sense of involvement and movement.

Colour was a key element in the project from the start and when Alsop proposed overall blue for the station it was immediately accepted at the top. Chairman Sir Wilfrid Newton had previously been Chairman of the Hong Kong MTR, which had several all blue mosaic-clad stations. This approach had been very successful at Hong Kong – giving otherwise very basic stations an air of richness and unity. The idea of having another such station in London appealed for its sense of connection and continuity. London Underground's Managing Director, Denis Tunnicliffe, was less sure and recalls thinking that 'the blue was over the top – not really our thing. But I let Roland build it'. Alsop believes that the use of colour was vital, helping to reinforce the sense of objects floating in a great void. The colour helps to break down the edges of the volume, adds to the mystery and enhances the sense of being not only in a space but in an event. The use of a wall of rich blue glass, lit from behind, is particularly effective. The non finito aspect of the ceiling area – like those of Canada Water and Southwark upper concourse – and the platform wall reflects Paoletti's Tuscan philosophy: 'If we cannot afford to do it properly as the architect wants it is better to leave it unfinished "in time" and design it accordingly.' In fact, Paoletti prefers it that way, and feels that it increases the feeling of abstract space and moderates any sense of preciousness or over-design – North Greenwich is as purposeful and functional a station as any on the line. Yet it has a quality – a sense of delight – which goes beyond the functional. As Lyall puts it: 'The sculptural potential of stainless steel, bare concrete, exposed ductwork and terrazzo – used with care and restraint – have resulted in bold aesthetic

statements which are also tough and hard-wearing.

It was always Roland Paoletti's intention that some stations would be more flamboyant than others, the high points of reference on the line. Like Stratford, Canary Wharf and Westminster, each with its own character, North Greenwich, with its colour and elegance, fulfils that hope perfectly, while staying true to the ideals of legibility and clarity common to the whole line.

The bus and Underground stations work well together, and before very long they will be at the heart of a new urban village – created by the JLE. As in the inter-war years, London is growing to meet the Underground. At North Greenwich, you find the millennium version of the transport interchanges built on the Piccadilly Line in the 1930s. The difference is that the architects have created an interchange with all the presence and excitement of a regional airport. This is regeneration in earnest.

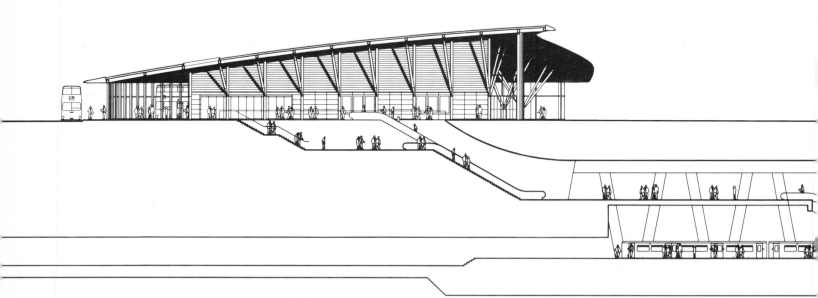

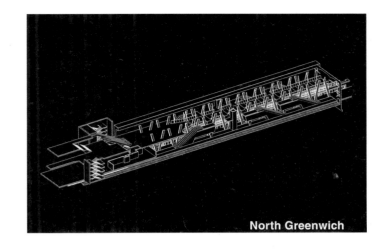

North Greenwich

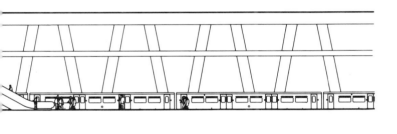

above and left
The station is located within a 358 metre-
(1,175 foot-) long box sunk into the
waterlogged soil. It is entered through a bus
station designed by Foster & Partners.

below
Built on the site of a vast gasworks, some
distance from historic Greenwich, North
Greenwich station serves the Millennium
Dome and the new 'urban village' being
developed on the peninsula.

opposite
A mid-eighteenth-century view of Greenwich
with the Isle of Dogs to the right and London
in the distance. What was once a village on
the outskirts of the capital now has a direct
tube link to its centre.

previous page
Illuminated by night, the bus station extends
its glazed wings to welcome the traveller.

left
Foster & Partners' bus station is a new
public transport hub for south-east London.
Its light and elegant form provides a contrast
to the emotional intensity of the
Underground station.

overleaf
The phalanx of entry gates at North
Greenwich reflects the sheer scale of this
station, serving the Millennium Dome and
the regenerated Greenwich Peninsula.

The unique character of North Greenwich lies in the contrast of stainless steel and blue mosaic, while the ceiling of the station is deliberately 'unfinished', with services frankly exposed.

Cobalt blue glass, backlit, is used as a wall cladding, producing intriguing reflections of escalators, trains and people.

Way out ↗

↖ Way out

PLEASE KEEP YOUR LUGGAGE WITH YOU
AT ALL TIMES

The use of strong colour at North Greenwich – albeit 'Underground blue' – contrasts with the grey and silver aesthetic of most of the other stations on the line.

The roof at North Greenwich is supported on 'V' formation columns, with the passenger concourse suspended from it.

canning town

Canning Town Station illustrates the JLE's role as an engine of regeneration. Its site, overshadowed by the elevated A13 trunk road, squeezed by Bow Creek (where the River Lea joins the Thames) and existing railway lines, and criss-crossed by high-voltage pylons, has a context of scrap yards, a margarine factory and mundane council housing across Silvertown Way. The Underground will transform this locale, achieving what existing, ill-connected surface links – the North London Line and the Docklands Light Railway (DLR) – could not.

Canning Town is a raw slice of London where reality verges on the surreal. Yet the station site has a history every bit as significant as Westminster or Southwark, intimately linked to Victorian Britain's role as 'the workshop of the world'. Here stood one of the great shipyards of the world, employing up to 6,000 people and producing, over the 66 years of its existence, up to 1,000 ships. The Thames Ironworks, Shipbuilding and Engineering Company (as it became known) was an integrated plant producing iron, the raw material for the ships of the future. It built ships for the Royal Navy and for foreign powers – HMS *Warrior*, the world's first 'ironclad' battleship, was constructed here. Other large iron structures fabricated here included the components for the Menai Straits and Tamar rail bridges and London's Westminster Bridge. The Thames Ironworks was a progressive employer, sponsoring leisure pursuits for its employees. Its football team quickly became one of the best in London and in 1900 it changed its name to West Ham United. 'The Hammers' went on to wider fame but the yard closed in 1912, a blow from which Canning Town never really recovered.

Troughton McAslan's station, bringing together the JLE, DLR and North London Line, is a beautiful and dynamic object, with more than a hint of a futuristic ship permanently beached alongside Silvertown Way. The contract was one of the last on the line to be awarded (in 1991), along with Stratford and West Ham, though Troughton McAslan had long been identified as a potential part of the JLE team and had bid, unsuccessfully, for Bermondsey. Jamie Troughton, who led the design team working for technical contractors Kenchington Ford, contrasts the 'calm and ordered' Stratford scheme (see pages 152–67) with the 'explosion of activity' which is expressed at Canning Town. 'The architecture is about capitalizing on the energy and excitement of the engineering', he says.

At Canning Town, the line, having crossed the river, finally emerges into daylight and runs alongside the North London Line for 3.5 kilometres (2 miles) to the terminus at Stratford. A link to both the North London Line and the DLR's Beckton branch (which opened in 1994) was always an objective, but there were major problems accommodating three systems on a narrow site with extraordinarily complex ground and surface conditions. Initially in fact, it was proposed that the old North London station remain where it was, north of the A13 and some way from the combined JLE/DLR station. The local authority had successfully campaigned for the inclusion of a station at Canning Town in the DLR system. It was determined to have this station directly linked to the tube and North London Line, and pushed London Underground to reconsider. The result was the integration of all three routes on the present site, together with a bus station designed for London Buses in a transport node and growth point for the far East End. It was the right decision, but it provided immense problems for the engineers and architects involved.

The approach to these problems produced the exhilarating solution embodied in the new station. When there were just two lines to be accommodated, the form of the station, as set out in the initial JLE diagram, was to be a ticket hall and concourse spanning over both sets of tracks. With the third line, this approach became impractical – the site was too narrow for six tracks and the only way that it could be implemented would be to close Silvertown Way, which was clearly impossible. The key move at Canning Town – a double-decker station – emerged, with the DLR now located above the JLE and the two levels linked by escalators. In fact, the station became not so much a double as a triple-decker, with the new booking hall serving all three lines underground in the 'belly' of the station. The station was, in effect, 'pushed into the ground'. There were good reasons for this. The high-voltage power line across the site could not, it was decided, be moved and there were rigorous provisions to ensure that no structure came within 6 metres (19 feet) of the power lines. The existence of the lines equally ruled out the use of cranes on the site – a serious practical issue. These issues compounded the existing problems of heavily waterlogged soil and the way in which the other rail services could operate while the JLE was being constructed. (The DLR was rerouted before it opened, though the North London Line had to close for a time.) A close collaboration between the architects, Malcolm Davidson of Kenchington Ford (subsequently WSP) and the JLE's own engineering and architectural team produced solutions which are functionally efficient, 'buildable', and visually striking – 'all done in the context of reporting to six clients', Troughton recalls.

A structural approach was developed, with pre-cast, V-shaped concrete column formations on the lower (JLE) level supporting the slab for the DLR platforms. The question was: how could it be assembled without cranes? Once the concourse box (with a 2 metre-/6½ feet-thick base slab) had been dug out, with diaphragm walls 22 metres (72 feet) deep and part of the slab for the JLE platforms on top, the 96 metre- (314 feet-) long DLR platform structure was moved into position horizontally, like a piece of Meccano, in 14.5-metre (47-feet) sections. The structural requirement is demanding, yet the means appear comparatively light, part of an imperative for legibility and clarity that is common to all the stations on the line. One of the great strengths of this station is the disinclination of the architects to embroider the work of the engineers. Only the striking, rather nautical-looking outriggers, which appear to support the covering of the DLR platforms, but are actually cosmetic, strike a slightly unconvincing note. Yet the station has a role beyond the purely operational, which perhaps justifies an evocative gesture of this sort.

With the superstructure complete, the station box could be constructed top-down. Getting natural light into the stations was one of the key elements in the JLE's brief to architects. At Canning Town, there is a top-lit concourse, north of the rail tracks, which provides a connection between bus and rail facilities. This is a generous gesture, like the connecting concourse at London Bridge; it is not a necessary element of the JLE station but a motion towards a better public realm. The concourse does not seem subterranean, but is a calm and civilized space that connects neatly with the bus station, also designed by Troughton McAslan, via escalators. It is assumed that most rail passengers (London Transport predict up to 10,000 during future rush-hour peaks) will enter the station this way. Canning Town is seen primarily as an interchange, a gateway to an area previously badly served by public transport and considered inaccessible and undesirable. The connecting concourse is clad in aluminium panels that subtly reflect the light. A second entry, at the west of the concourse, provides mainly for local users who arrive on foot. Outside is a small square, walled against traffic noise – a defensive move, perhaps, though the architects were anxious not to create a 'fortress'. They succeeded so well that the complex of buildings has a remarkable delicacy of appearance.

Canning Town station is the setting for one of the few art works installed on the JLE. Jamie Troughton felt strongly, as did West Ham United Football Club, that there should be a memory in the building of the Thames Ironworks, which had been such a monumental element in the area's history. Nobody can remember the works, closed before the First World War, yet its legend survives, as did West Ham United. The club funded a memorial to the operation from which it had sprung nearly a century ago. The letter-cutter Richard Kindersley was commissioned to cut an inscription about the history of the ironworks and club in the concrete around the staircase, with a great slab of iron taken from the hull of HMS *Warrior* when the ship was restored, as a centrepiece. It was a daunting job. Kindersley was used to working in solid stone but concrete, with its mix of ingredients, is far less predictable. There was no room for errors as the concrete panels could not be replaced. It took Kindersley and four assistants three weeks to complete the inscription – 'cover it with calligraphy', Troughton had urged.

The work stirred a lot of interest locally, especially when East End-born Dr George Carey, Archbishop of Canterbury, came to unveil it. The appeal to local pride was deliberate. Canning Town has little charm and no place in the recent history of London or Britain. But the advent of the JLE will change its destiny. The new station, looking as if it could sail away, such is its elegant grace, is rooted in place and history, but it is also a resource for a bright future.

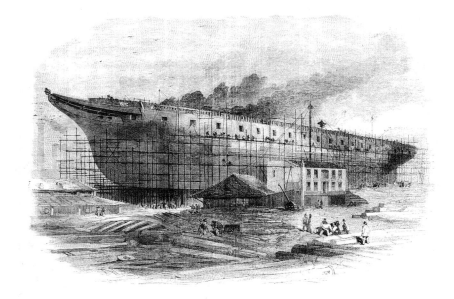

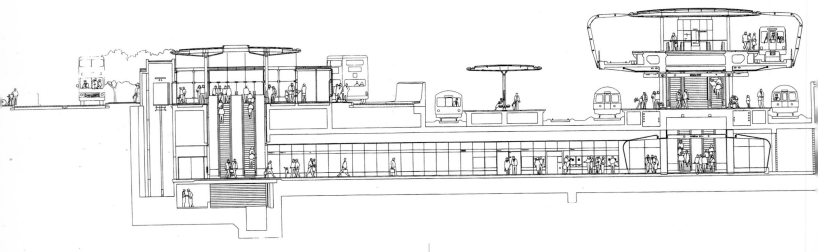

previous pages
The bus station is a light and transparent place, a vital link from the Underground to the hinterland of the far East End.

left
A glass stair canopy leading to the bus station reflects the architects' aim to allow as much natural light as possible into the station.

opposite
An escalator link connects the bus station to the Underground concourse level.

The main station concourse is toplit, with striking views up to the platforms above.

overleaf
The double-decker structure carrying the DLR tracks above the Jubilee Line is the most striking element in the Canning Town project and assembling it was a major engineering challenge.

west ham

The setting of Canning Town Station may be bleak, but that of West Ham, the next station down the line is, with its deteriorating Thirties red brick, presented no less an architectural challenge. It is a challenge to which the practice of Joanna van Heyningen and Birkin Haward responded with gusto, producing a building that they see as the key to 'making a place'. Holden did just this in the new suburbs between the wars – his stations became the pivot for future development – and it is to Holden that van Heyningen and Haward looked for inspiration.

Yet West Ham Station is very far from pastiche or pure revival of a past style. 'Our work is in a tradition, but it is not "traditional"', the architects insist. 'We want to look beyond fashion and make something timeless, calm and dignified, which will look good 30 years from now. We are passionate about creating buildings that will wear well. Underground stations have to be tough – Holden understood that. This is a working station, not a millennium landmark.'

Together with Canning Town and Stratford (the other surface stations), West Ham was one of the last of the JLE's architectural commissions. All three are vital links in the developing public transport system for London's East End, proof that the JLE is about regeneration and social gain and not just a business-oriented Docklands link. The existing District/Metropolitan Line station was to be simply refurbished – the Underground had been running trains over the Upminster route since the turn of the century, though the stations only passed formally into its hands in 1969. British Rail, as successor to the London, Tilbury & Southend Railway, retained the fast tracks, but none of the Fenchurch Street trains stopped at West Ham. There was also a station for the North London Line at a lower level, separated from the Underground by a major road, and it

was inevitable that the JLE platforms would be developed alongside this. The new station would provide a proper link between all the services. (As the JLE project developed, in fact, it was decided to reopen West Ham as a stop on the Fenchurch Street Line, so reinforcing its value as an interchange.)

The existing Underground ticket hall, located under the tracks, was small and dismal. The diagram adopted for the new station was to build a new, much enlarged concourse incorporating the old ticket hall, to serve all train operators and to connect it to the North London Line and JLE by a bridge across the road, a sub-surface link having been considered and rejected. For the architects – 'we were sub-contractors, not the lead designers' – this was a fast job: 1,000 drawings in 27 weeks. But van Heyningen and Haward thought hard about the image of the station as well as about its operational performance. While it would, above all, be an interchange (local traffic was predicted as just 7 per cent of the total), the station needed to address the shabby streets in which it stood and maybe assume a quasi-civic role as the only public building in the immediate neighbourhood. Provision of shops and kiosks would strengthen it as a local focus and also bring in useful rental income – as had generally been included in the new stations of the inter-war years. There was to be a small square in front of the station, another civic gesture, overlooked by an arcaded entrance.

Van Heyningen and Haward's chosen palette of materials was brick, glass blocks and concrete – with no more trimmings than any other station on the line. Using tried and tested materials was vital to such a fast-track project. By keeping details simple, the requisite results were more likely to be achieved, whatever the contractors' skills. The architects also advocated a 'realistic' view of services, which might change many times in the life of the station. (Major additions, not always well-integrated with the architecture, occurred here and on other JLE stations, even before they opened to passengers.) Flexibility, durability and low-maintenance requirements were the ingredients of a good-value building – West Ham was by far the cheapest of all the stations on the JLE, and in effect subsidized the more elaborate approach of Canning Town.

A 'kit of parts' approach was seen as particularly appropriate to securing these objectives. The station is designed on a 6-metre (19-feet) grid. The basic element is a 275 x 275-mm (10 x 10-inch) *in situ* concrete column, generally enclosed in brickwork, but circular when it is freestanding. The columns are the basis of a structural matrix in which the public spaces are formed. The bridge is the vital link. It is made a more pleasant place by day, and a more secure place after dark, by the use of glass bricks, so that people walking across it can be clearly seen from the street below. At night, lighting gives the station a 'glow', equally welcoming to the early-morning commuter in winter. The C.H. James/Holden-designed Oakwood (1933) on the Piccadilly Line can be seen as a model for van Heyningen and Haward. Its language of brickwork and concrete beams finds an echo at West Ham.

The architects' dictum about services was reflected in the very generous, highly accessible ducts that extend around all parts of the station. They should cope with all eventualities, though no architect can predict the future of a building. An important element of the West Ham concourse, the view down from the bridge and adjacent galleries, has been badly compromised by galvanized steel grilles put in at the insistence of railway inspectors.

From the JLE platforms at West Ham is a view of the Millennium Dome, symbol of an ongoing renaissance for the Docklands and East End. The station has no pretensions to being a monument, but it does lift and refresh a jaded quarter, providing an element of architectonic strength and reassuring permanence amidst the roar of traffic and rattle of trains. Whether it marks a return to an old tradition or is a model for an unpretentious, high-value Underground architecture of the twenty-first century is open to debate. But it rises above its mundane surroundings, like the great brick churches of the nineteenth century, the 'building of integrity, dignity and lasting value' that its architects set out to create.

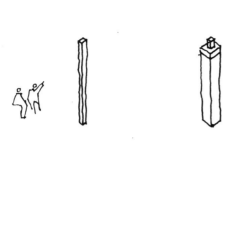

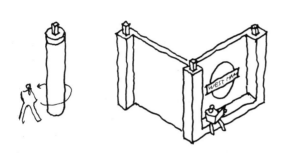

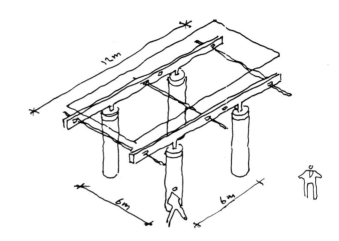

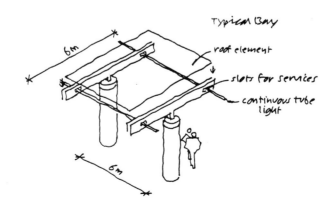

Typical Bay

roof element

slots for services

continuous tube light

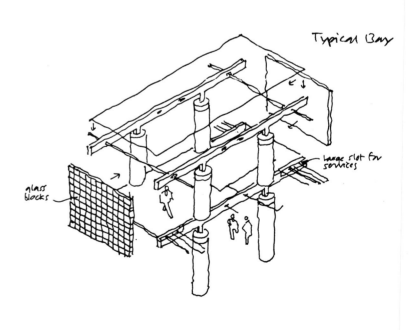

Typical Bay

glass blocks

large slot for services

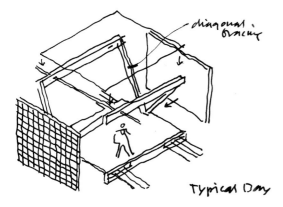

diagonal bracing

Typical Day

right
An early nineteenth-century view of West Ham showing one of the characteristic water-mills that once dotted the River Lea as far as Stratford.

West Ham Station was conceived as a 'kit of parts' structure, formed out of concrete columns and beams infilled with brick and glass.

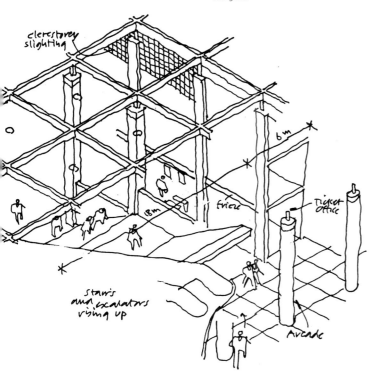

clerestorey slighting

6m

18m

frieze

Ticket office

stairs and escalators rising up

Arcade

The station forms a civic focus in an unprepossessing district.

overleaf
The bridge which links the booking hall with the platforms is the vital link at West Ham – glass bricks, with panels of clear glass, are used to provide ample natural light.

In terms of its materials, regular grid plan and approach to space, West Ham Station looks back to the work of Holden, though it is a reinterpretation, not a pastiche, of the Underground tradition.

stratford

Stratford is the end of the line for the JLE. The town centre, which the critic Ian Nairn considered to be 'the real centre of the East End', has suffered from much mediocre development over the last 30 years, but retains a distinctive identity and considerable vitality. The railway is a powerful presence – the swathes of freight yards help to reinforce Stratford's continuing sense of separation from the rest of East London. The Eastern Counties Railway (later Great Eastern) came through in the 1840s, erecting a locomotive building works here (which survived until 1963) and still carries large numbers of commuters into London from East Anglia. The Underground – the extended Central Line – arrived in Stratford in 1946, sharing the mainline station. The period was one of austerity and the Underground's facilities were no more impressive than the Great Eastern's. When the Docklands Light Railway came to Stratford, it made use of an unprepossessing section of the above-ground station. Such integration of transport facilities as existed was rudimentary and seemingly incidental. The JLE provided the opportunity to revolutionize Stratford's unimpressive and inconvenient public transport interchange and to contribute to the regeneration of the town centre. The expectation that the Channel Tunnel Rail Link would reach Stratford early this century added to a general air of renewal and confidence, with the railway once more a potent force.

Running at surface level alongside the North London Line, the JLE arrives in Stratford to the south of the mainline station. Its open-air platforms, with attached staff accommodation, were designed by Troughton McAslan and are, in architect Jamie Troughton's words, 'calm and ordered'. Booking offices and other passenger amenities for all services were to be contained within a separate terminus building, providing an interchange between mainline, Central Line, JLE and North London Line services. A limited design competition for the latter was won by Chris Wilkinson Architects (led by Jim Eyre) in July 1994 – the perceived success of the practice's nearby depot, then under construction, may have influenced the decision.

The first challenge had been to involve Railtrack in the project and to fund it on an appropriate scale: European Union and other development funds were successfully tapped. Even when a deal had been achieved by London Underground, very basic design decisions remained to be taken, principally related to the disparity of levels between the mainline, JLE and North London Line platforms, and the way in which interconnection between the systems could be achieved. Wilkinson's strategy, developed with engineers Acer Consulting and Ove Arup & Partners, was to provide a two-level concourse with a mezzanine, serviced by escalators and lifts, that crossed the North London Line – a singular feature of the station is that the North London Line runs within the terminal building at ground level. From the mezzanine, there are views out to the mainline and Central Line platforms.

The issue of how the new building could address the old mainline station was complex. The only logical way to access the mainline platforms from the new concourse was by means of a broad tunnel boldly cut underneath – this was built out of concrete box sections and rolled into position, the platforms remaining in use throughout. The initial brief had led the architects to visually integrate the old Great Eastern station. 'We turned the terminus around to address not the station, but the town', says Wilkinson. 'We were taking something of a gamble.' But this strategy facilitated interchange with the new bus station and the creation of a decent public space around it. It also made the station the clear focus of the town centre, a real and dignified point of arrival and a local landmark.

The interior of the new 'regional station' has none of the structural complexity of Wilkinson's earlier depot. The clean and simple aesthetic is deliberate, a counterpoint to the activity generated by milling commuters. The roof came first, sketched freehand in pencil and then developed with computer technology and subjected to rigorous performance analysis. Its asymmetrical curve is rooted back to the embankment of the Victorian railway and embedded in a solid new concrete base, from which the ribs of the roof spring at mezzanine level. It soars up to the sheer glass entrance façade, daringly propped on slim long-span steel trusses and incorporating a lightweight, rod-hung glazing system developed by the architects in consultation with glass manufacturer Pilkington. The completed building is filled with daylight, but the dynamic angle of the south-facing façade and the use of oversailing louvres counteracts solar gain and glare to create a modulated light – artificial lighting is only needed on the dullest days. Energy economies were part of the design agenda from the start, with consultant Loren Butt advising on ways in which conventional concentrations of plant could be eliminated. The roof is a double-skinned construction, the deep void within it acting as a thermal generator in warm weather, pulling cooling breezes through the building. (Smoke can also be extracted at roof level in the case of a fire.) The concourse is naturally ventilated, an 'inside/outside' space in the tradition of earlier railway stations, but with something of the glamour of modern air terminals. A high degree of transparency is a vital element in the scheme. The building has a particularly strong presence after dark, when carefully controlled lighting reflected off stainless-steel cladding turns it into a glowing jewel-like box. The use of glass balustrades and lifts adds to the permeability of the interior.

Wilkinson's station successfully combines the roles of transport interchange and civic landmark. Such is the impact of the architectural statement that the unresolved problems that remain – the awkwardness of the North London Line's incursion into the concourse and the continuing gulf between the Underground and mainline platforms, which may one day be filled by CrossRail tracks – do not undermine the achievement. (Nor is the Docklands Light Railway properly integrated, despite earlier proposals for it to be moved to connect directly to the new terminal.)

Commissioned late in the JLE project (it was built in 1996–8), Stratford Station faced additional problems because of the involvement of several clients (the Stratford Development Partnership Ltd and Newham Council as well as London Underground). The building reflects priorities other than those of rail operations. This is a stylish monument that makes a statement about the renaissance of old town centres and of public transport, and points optimistically towards the closer integration of transport systems currently suffering from the absence of a clear overall direction. If it has mannerisms, these are forgivable in the context of the brief. A few years ago, a new railway station of this quality would have been inconceivable anywhere in Britain. It was the catalyst of the JLE that made it possible.

left
The first rail link to Stratford came when the viaduct was constructed for the Eastern Counties Railway in 1837.

opposite
The form of the station reflects its context between the town centre and the busy tracks. The North London/Silverlink service runs directly through the concourse area, necessitating a mezzanine level.

below left
Sections showing how the glass front (top) and double-skinned roof (bottom) were designed to control lighting and ventilation.

overleaf
The new station at Stratford serves mainline, Silverlink, and Docklands Light Railway trains as well as the Jubilee Line. The concourse is an impressive public space, addressing the town centre.

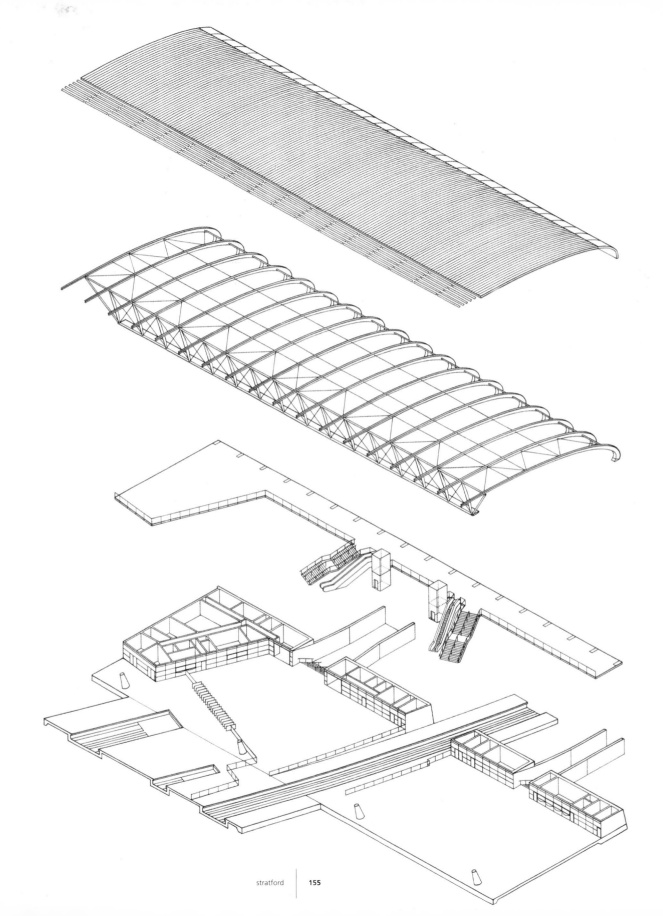

The sheer glass façade incorporates innovative glazing technology to achieve maximum transparency and lightness. A carefully considered lighting strategy contributes to the 'jewel box' effect of the station by night.

opposite
The transparency of the station helps to blur
the boundaries between inside and outside.

right
The highly glazed concourse rarely requires
artificial light during daytime. Oversailing
louvres help to reduce solar gain and glare.

overleaf
The scale of the concourse at Stratford is that
of a city terminal. Its transparent glazed
façade looks out over 'the capital of the
East End'.

The roof of the concourse at Stratford is the generator of the entire building, springing forward from the Victorian railway embankment and soaring up to the entrance façade.

The Jubilee Line platforms at Stratford, by
Troughton McAslan, are in the open air, with
service buildings in a strictly rational manner.

stratford depot

Stratford Market Depot was a highlight of the JLE, and a potent image of the renaissance of transport architecture, even before it was completed. A striking computer-generated aerial view of the building issued in 1994 struck a particular chord with critics and the public, perhaps because the great curved roof seemed to echo those of the big Victorian railway termini. As executed (built in two years, the depot was completed in April 1996 and opened in 1998 as the first JLE building to be brought into use), the reality is as striking as the electronic vision, a 'supershed' for the new railway age, rather than a universal high-tech, rational 'box'. Yet it is inaccessible to the public, set on a secure, landlocked site – indeed, the best views are obtained by passengers travelling on the JLE between Stratford and West Ham.

The need for a maintenance and repair depot to complement that at Neasden, at the northern end of the Jubilee Line, was identified early on in the project. There was a clear functional requirement, but only the determination of the JLE's architectural team produced what Roland Paoletti had seen as an 'educative' building. The depot is, perhaps, the spiritual heart of the JLE and reflects the application of high-design standards to all aspects of the project.

The history of the 8.9-hectare (22-acre) site, occupied by a wholesale market established in 1879, certainly had a spiritual dimension. Stratford's Cistercian abbey (established in 1135; dissolved in 1538) had long vanished without trace, but excavations revealed extensive remains, including a monastic cemetery from which 683 skeletons were exhumed for reburial at Mount St Bernard Abbey, Leicestershire. The imperative to protect the archaeology largely determined the layout of the site, with buildings concentrated on the western

half, where there were no restrictions on piling, and the remainder occupied by open sidings for stabling trains.

Chris Wilkinson Architects was appointed to design the depot in June 1991, following an unsuccessful bid for London Bridge Station. The practice met Paoletti's criterion of being, at that time, relatively small but already critically noticed. It worked with structural engineers Acer Consulting Ltd, led by Richard Fenton, to produce a proposal that met the complex brief for the project.

Railway maintenance depots are traditionally utilitarian structures, often with poor working conditions. Wilkinson's team, led by partner-in-charge Jim Eyre, shared Paoletti's vision of something better. In his book *Supersheds* of 1996, Chris Wilkinson previewed a new generation of buildings that would 'move beyond the cool box and explore the image and potential of lightweight structures, high-performance cladding and glazing systems, servicing arrangements and plan forms.' The assumption at Stratford was that one building would contain all the uses required: offices, staff amenities, stores, an electrical sub-station and control room as well as the core activities of cleaning, maintaining and repairing trains. The architects, however, proposed a 'family' of buildings with the subsidiary activities outside the shed, a strategy that simplified servicing and fire safety provisions. The buildings along the western edge of the shed are designed to address a specific brief – the offices, for example, are air-conditioned, with good daylighting and raised floors.

The basic requirement for the maintenance shed was that it should provide a completely enclosed space for entire trains on dead-straight tracks. Given the placing of the depot on the site, almost at right angles to the track, this posed some problems and produced the distinctive form of a skewed parallelogram rather than a rectangle, with the roof line cut off at 30 degrees. This was, in any case, the first JLE building, a symbol and harbinger of what was to come. There was an expectation that economy and efficiency would be combined with a striking expression of purpose. The architects and engineers were able to develop a highly efficient structure, both elegant and relatively modest in cost, which provided a high-quality working environment.

The shed is 190 metres (623 feet) long, 100 metres (328 feet) across (St Pancras Station has a clear span of 89 metres/291 feet), with space for up to 11 trains to be serviced at any one time. A clear span was not required (and could not easily be achieved on such a shallow curve), though internal supports were to be kept to a minimum, and there was no excuse for structural gymnastics. Instead, standardized components were used to good effect to create what is really a hybrid structure. The space is divided by two rows of concrete-filled steel columns, set on a 42 x 18-metre (137 x 59-feet) grid, which act as 'trees' (in the tradition of Norman Foster's Stansted terminal and of Wilkinson's atrium roof in Ipswich for Willis Corroon) supporting the dynamic diagrid roof structure, itself a natural reflection of the parallelogram plan but evocative, perhaps deliberately, of Pier Luigi Nervi's famous aircraft hangers at Orvieto and Torre del Lago. The vast roof is formed of 9 metre- (29 feet-) long, 2.4 metre- (8 feet-) deep, tubular steel trusses fixed with friction joints to create a space structure. At the perimeter, it sits on V-shaped steel columns. The roof covering is upstanding seamed aluminium sheeting. Rainwater is directed into very generous (800-mm/31-inch) perimeter gutters on the long sides of the shed, a low-maintenance strategy

that helped to convince London Transport of the essential logic and economy of the scheme. The side walls are clad in profiled steel sheeting with a silver finish. The north elevation, through which trains enter, is fully glazed above the level of the doors, while the south elevation is clad in KalWall, a fibreglass panel system that produces an attractive, diffused light while controlling solar gain.

Good natural light was a requirement of the brief and clerestory glazing and the long slits of rooflights (which open for ventilation and smoke dispersal in the case of fire) are part of the daylighting strategy. The clear and calm light within the building is one of its most significant qualities. Although the depot is unimpeachably 'functional', it nonetheless offers a quality of delight uncommon within the context of industrial architecture – in the line, indeed, of the legendary sheds designed by Norman Foster (for whom Chris Wilkinson worked for a time) and Richard Rogers. The apparent delicacy of the building belies its robust nature. The use of a gentle green hue for the steel structure – inspired by the very robust Runcorn Bridge over the River Mersey – softens its impact and heightens the illusion that, rows of columns notwithstanding, it is floating in space.

Staff at the Stratford Depot contrast working conditions there to those in older depots where inspection pits are used to examine trains and are confined, dirty and potentially dangerous spaces. The central section of the Stratford shed is depressed, so that the tracks are elevated above floor level for easy inspection. Good natural light, controlled temperatures (the shed is thoroughly insulated and heated in cold weather) and the elimination of internal subdivisions and messy corners produce an agreeable workplace of which there is every incentive to maintain well.

Everything is made for hard wear, but good looks are equally an objective – the freestanding toilet pods within the shed (which were subsequently selected as a Millennium Product) reflect that balance. Brightly painted lifting equipment sits happily within the space.

Stratford Market Depot is as powerful an expression of the radical agenda underlying the JLE project as any of the stations on the line – more so, in some respects, since it is a showpiece that few outsiders will ever see. As in the stations, space is generous, but in both cases the rationale is practical rather than rhetorical and safety is a high priority. The most spectacular views of the interior are gained from the mezzanine walkway across the north end of the shed – not a luxury, but a much-used staff circulation route. It provides access to the circular control room (from where access to the shed and sidings is monitored), a little gem of a structure in its own right with frameless glazing to facilitate a clear view of train movements.

The depot is the central element in a 'campus' of buildings, all – right down to a bicycle shed – carefully detailed and appropriate to their various uses, an apt environment for a skilled workforce on which the Underground depends. They are grouped alongside the shed, creating an oasis of order within a sprawling site on the rundown fringe of Stratford town centre. The nineteenth-century railway created modern Stratford, extinguishing its semi-rural isolation and creating a raw, even bleak new landscape of tracks and marshalling yards, through which the final section of the JLE passes. Wilkinson's depot seems to look back beyond the age of industry. Its associations with the age of steam are superficial. When the depot won the *Financial Times* Architecture at Work Award in 1997,

it was compared to a modern cathedral. The depot has a cool economy which is, in fact, more in the spirit of the great Cistercian churches – one of which stood on this very site. This is a building in the 'functional tradition' – closer in spirit to nineteenth-century railway buildings than the more consciously styled Underground tradition of Holden and others. There is no attempt at grandiloquence – the grandeur arises from the sense of purpose – and a rigorous disinclination to flaunt the structural achievement involved. This is one of the outstanding working buildings of the late twentieth century and it has rightly established the standing of its architects as one of the leading British practices today.

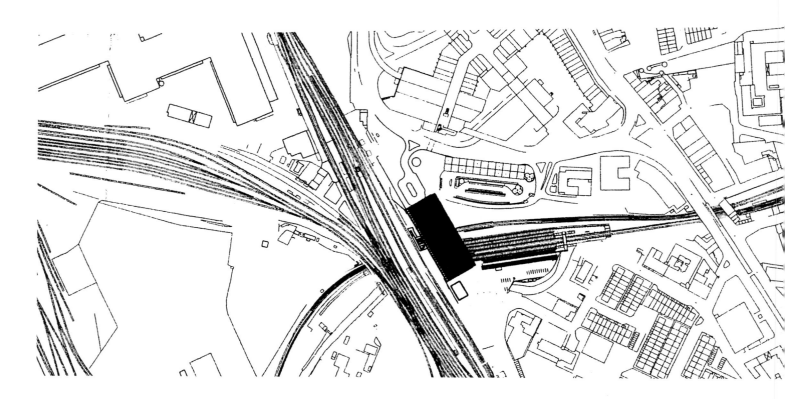

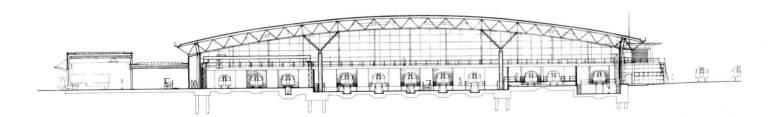

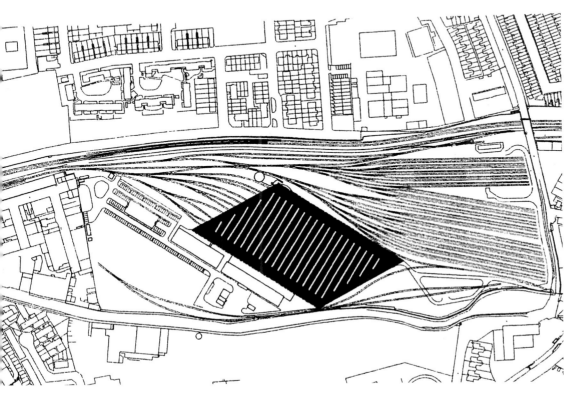

opposite
Stratford depot was built on the site of a Cistercian abbey (now totally destroyed), the remains of which were recorded in this nineteenth-century watercolour.

above and overleaf
The depot is a 'supershed', with intriguing echoes of the great railway termini of the nineteenth century.

left
Constraints of the site led to the distinctive parallelogram shape of the depot.

The diagrid roof structure reflects the parallelogram plan of the depot and is designed to admit generous but controlled amounts of natural light.

The north elevation, through which trains enter the depot, is fully glazed. An elegant little control centre monitors movement in and out of the building.

overleaf
The interior of Stratford Depot has real grandeur, but this is a building which the traveller never enters – it is a workplace.

components

Attention to detail is part of the legendary tradition of the London Underground. Back in 1930, however, Frank Pick, visiting the fine new Sudbury Town Station, found 'too many afterthoughts' – intrusive 'tombstone' notice-boards, random wiring, vending machines 'dumped down' on the platforms and lighting crudely screwed on to concrete. 'There is an entire lack of design and orderly workmanship', he wrote.

Given the proliferation of legislation and regulation imposed on the Underground in more recent years, the task of the JLE's architects and designers in avoiding such 'afterthoughts', or at least minimizing their impact, was all the harder. All products had to achieve a high level of quality, durability and ease of maintenance in the hostile station and tunnel environments. Systems were devised to ease installation and future fit-outs by station operators. A practical, rather than purely aesthetic, case for redesign had to be made. London Underground has developed a standard range of station fittings that are used throughout the rest of the system. While the architectural programme of the JLE encouraged controlled diversity, the fit-out of stations had to express a common, line-wide identity, particularly at platform level. A dedicated component design team, led by Julian Maynard, was set up by Roland Paoletti to tackle this task.

As a result of the team's success, a number of the innovations made on the JLE may influence the look of the Underground in the next century. The standard JLE booking office is certainly a model for the future – distinctive, because of the use of blue glass, highly secure and designed to present a neat public façade while offering good working spaces for staff. After buying a ticket, passengers pass through a redesigned gateline,

supervised from a 'glap' (gateline attendance point) – a vast improvement on the 'sentry box' formerly used. A similar approach was taken to the other products and internal fit-out contracts. The ticket office, station operations room and gateline barriers were grouped together ensuring a consistent level of design and installation. Issues of passenger safety, comfort and mobility were also addressed in the introduction of extra lifts, all with redesigned, easy-to-use interiors. Another safety feature, new to London Underground, was the addition of platform edge doors. The doors, which incorporate glass, stainless steel and aluminium, were designed to reflect a transportation aesthetic rather than a strictly architectural one.

The use of a services boom on the platforms, to gather together lights, security cameras, signage and PA speakers – all finished in the same colour to promote consistency – is another valuable innovation, countering the spread of untidy additions to the stations. While standard London Underground signage had to be retained, a new range of brackets was designed to hold wiring and other extraneous elements. To echo the design quality of the rest of the JLE components, the London Underground roundel – normally tin plate – was produced in a chunkier cast aluminium and either mounted on platform tunnel walls or, on open platforms, positioned as a freestanding element.

Seating is not standard across the line. Instead, it has been selected to suit the look of each station for example the glass seating designed by Ian Ritchie Architects at Bermondsey (see page 81). One of the seating components to be used throughout the line, the elegant aluminium platform lean-bar, is a particularly enterprising design.

previous page
The lightweight grey powder-coated aluminium platform lean-bar epitomizes the high standard of component design on the JLE.

opposite top and bottom
The traditional small ticket window was replaced by a full-height modular glass façade, incorporating signage. Internally everything from ticket machines to cash trays was redesigned.

opposite centre
The gateline attendance point (or glap) was designed to provide staff with good all-round vision and a secure working environment.

right
Platform edge doors were installed in nine of the JLE stations, providing a safety feature that is an innovation on the Underground.
   Much of the seating, such as this example at Canada Water, was custom-designed for each station. The freestanding roundel is cast aluminium, another development by the JLE component design team.

opposite and far right top
Seven kilometres of booms weave their way through concourses, down escalators and along platforms carrying lights, speakers, cameras and signage.

top right
The booms are made of extruded aluminium sections held together by cast brackets. These are supported by tapered steel struts which are connected to the tunnel lininings.

centre and bottom right
Designs for speakers and cast aluminium safety barriers for escalators illustrate the JLE's aim to provide technologically advanced safety features that also complement the station interiors.

far right bottom
The JLE stations required 120 new escalators, providing an opportunity for all the related safety equipment, speakers, lights, signs and barriers to be updated and redesigned.

service
structures

EESCAPE AND VENT SHAFTS

Tunnels are a common feature of most surface railways. In the days of steam traction, they were noisome places, though the use of vertical vent shafts did something to disperse the smoke. When the first underground railway was built in London in the 1860s, the problems were more difficult, since shafts could not be dug at random in the dense fabric of the capital. The problem was resolved by the use of compressors on the locomotives that allowed smoke to be held in tanks and released at regular intervals along the line – which was, in any case, partly open to the air. When the first deep tube lines were constructed, vent shafts were still necessary to equalize air pressure in the tunnels, while escape and emergency shafts also became standard features of the system.

These essentially practical devices rarely demanded architectural treatment – an exception was Erith & Terry's Victoria Line vent shaft in Islington, which was given a cladding appropriate to its sensitive location. In line with its broader architectural programme, the JLE has treated escape and vent shafts as a design challenge. Vent and emergency access points are provided at each station and also at 1-kilometre intervals between stations. A further series of subsidiary structures was the result of the need for transformer sub-stations at various points along the line – again, the opportunity was taken to give these functional buildings an architectural form and to respond to planning pressure for an appropriate approach.

opposite
Ventilation escape shaft and traction sub-station at Canada Water.

Storeys Gate Headworks and Lodge, Birdcage Walk, Westminster

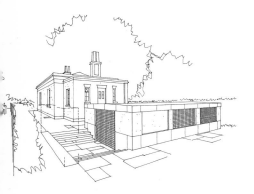

The need for a JLE ventilation and escape shaft on the east side of St James's Park posed the problem of integrating a new industrial structure into the sensitive and carefully protected context of a royal park. The project, designed by van Heyningen and Haward, was subject to close scrutiny from English Heritage and Westminster planners, not least because the site adjoined a listed lodge ascribed to John Nash, occupied by the Royal Parks Police.

Fortuitously, the police wanted to extend their premises, with a large locker room for staff attending major public functions such as the Trooping of the Colour, and this extension, which has been constructed entirely below ground, was included within the JLE project. The JLE escape stair and ventilation supply is contained within a discreet housing in the garden of the lodge, 1.6 metres (5.2 feet) high and faced in Flemish bond London stock brick on a Portland stone base, reflecting the materials of the lodge itself. Gates and grilles are of bronze. The lodge itself has been cleaned and repaired and surrounding fences and hedges restored.

The essence of this scheme is its discretion, yet the new building is a little gem, built in traditional materials – recalling Erith & Terry's elegant 'Temple of the Winds' ventilation shaft in Gibson Square, Islington – the only interesting piece of architecture generated by the Victoria Line.

Redcross Way Sub-station, Southwark

Designed by Weston Williamson, the sub-station is located some distance from London Bridge Station in an area that is being rapidly regenerated. The adjoining vacant site is likely to be developed for housing. The sub-station contains two huge transformers, which require nothing more than a secure container with good ventilation and occasional access for maintenance. Weston Williamson's first instinct was to give the building a strikingly contemporary look, with the ventilation grilles being a prominent feature. Southwark planners, however, wanted a more solid appearance. The final design is in the functional tradition of the nineteenth century, suitably updated, very straightforward and hardwearing, and executed in classic London stock brick. The rhythm of the main façade represents an attempt to express the disposition of the hardware inside the building.

Druid Street Shaft, Southwark

Ian Ritchie Architects designed six shafts between London Bridge and Canary Wharf, characterized by sculptural forms that articulate their essentially functional character – the movement of air is a theme. Initially, the idea was to create a 'family' of structures, but the pressure for a site-specific approach produced more diversity than was first envisaged. A range of heavy-duty materials was used, including a variety of concrete mixes. At Druid Street, near Tower Bridge, the shaft, plus a number of plantrooms, is slotted under the historic London Bridge–Greenwich railway viaduct. Railway arches are often put to practical use, but rarely with this degree of panache. Big steel louvres are recessed into the arches and sub-divided by vertical steel blade walls. Exit gates, for use in emergency, are formed from close-mesh steel grilles and read very much as an insertion – the cleaned and restored interior of the arches can be glimpsed through them. All steel plate is finished with a blue epoxy paint. A line of blue fluorescent lighting gives the louvres a night-time glow.

Ben Smith Way Shaft, Bermondsey

The architects were faced with the difficult task here of locating an escape and ventilation shaft close to a residential development next to Bermondsey Station, in an area occupied by communal gardens and garages. Any surface building had to be kept as small as possible, combining security with good looks. Ian Ritchie Architects managed to compress most of the plant beneath a new raised garden. The shaft is contained within a curving wall of smooth concrete, supporting a trellis and fruit trees. Replacement garages for residents are accommodated beneath the landscape.

Culling Road Shaft, Rotherhithe

The Culling Road shaft/plantroom building is an intriguing and enigmatic incident in the harsh landscape around the Rotherhithe Tunnel. The thematic expression of air movement is the key to the external composition – a series of concentric rings of increasing diameter. The building is clad in 2-mm copper sheet, arranged in panels and fixed between projecting horizontal stainless-steel angles that wrap around the ground-level plantrooms. The copper panels have been treated to encourage differential weathering and have a pleasingly uneven appearance. A projecting concrete blade wall expresses the division between the ventilation zone and the main shaft access point. Night-time illumination dramatizes the building and provides added security.

Durands Wharf Shaft, Rotherhithe

This shaft is located in a small park close to Rotherhithe Street and the designs seek to respond to the precious green setting. Two intersecting curved concrete walls form an outer enclosure to the plant and equipment yards, appearing to emerge from the ground and suggesting that they are the extrusion of a larger subterranean structure. The ventilation intake/exhaust is formed by an inverted cone of cable mesh inserted between the concrete walls and an elliptical stainless-steel roof. Great care was taken with the finish of the concrete, which has been surface-ground to expose a black basalt aggregate and to give an irregular look.

Pioneer Wharf Shaft / Downtown Road Shaft, Canada Water

These two escape shafts share a common design, though their locations are very different (Pioneer Wharf Shaft is shown above). The exteriors are treated as a monolith

executed in black basalt concrete. The perimeter walls gently curve in plan and the roof is formed as a shallow dome. A freestanding miniature monolith provides a separate enclosure for fire brigade inlet valves.

Stephenson Street Sub-stations, West Ham

Two linked sub-stations were required to convert the incoming 132-kilovolt main supply into 22 kilovolts for use on the JLE. Van Heyningen and Haward addressed the brief in the spirit of their designs for the nearby West Ham Station. The sub-stations are prominently sited and the architects felt strongly that the 'horrible tin sheds' which have become common on the Underground in recent years would not do. Their interest was in 'the long tradition of functional buildings that communicate, often in a monumental way, the sense of powerful forces at work within' – Birkin Haward cites Peter Behren's AEG factory in Berlin and H.B. Creswell's factory in Chester as examples of this manner. In a modest way, the West Ham sub-stations adopt a similarly monumental approach. The materials are commonplace – an *in situ* concrete frame, bricks and glass blocks – but the effect has a quiet authority. This is an economical restatement of the approach used, for example, by E. Vincent Harris in his splendid tramway sub-station of 1907 on Islington's Upper Street.

3

conclusion

Angela Carter's novel *Wise Children* (1991) relates the story of two women born on the 'wrong' (that is, the south) side of the Thames. For Carter, London is 'two cities divided by a river'. The Thames is a constant presence in the literature of London from the Middle Ages onwards and is mostly a benign, even paternal presence – 'Sweet Thames! run softly…', as the poet Edmund Spenser wrote. The fact of the river as a great divide has been taken for granted until very recently. Over the last two decades, however, its inevitability has been increasingly challenged. 'London turns its back on the river, yet it is, in embryo, the capital's greatest public amenity… potentially linking the prosperous north and the depressed south', argued Richard Rogers.[1] One of the most significant achievements of the era of Thatcherism – its flip side, you might say, engineered by the interventionist politician Michael Heseltine – was the regeneration of London's Docklands under the LDDC. If questionable in its social and economic priorities – it produced architecture and urban planning that mirrored its free-market triumphalism – the Docklands revival worked to the extent that it began the process of resuscitating and renewing the vast area of London east of Tower Bridge. The East Thames Corridor initiative, later renamed the Thames Gateway and another Heseltine strategy, followed on from what the LDDC had achieved, aiming to spread the benefits of regeneration socially and geographically, and to involve local communities and local politicians in a way that the LDDC failed to do. At the beginning of the twenty-first century, it is in the East End and Docklands – the boroughs of Tower Hamlets, Newham, Hackney, Southwark and Greenwich – that the new London of the millennium is being created. Newham alone is planning the

regeneration of 485 hectares (1,200 acres) of brownfield land. With the advent of London's new strategic authority and mayor, the old preconceptions are dead.

The JLE will be at the centre of the next great phase of London's continuing renewal. The idea of the JLE as a lifeline for Canary Wharf dies hard – and indeed, that mission undeniably played a part in its genesis. London Transport's view of the JLE was, however, always far broader: the JLE was seen as an extension of what the Underground had been doing for a century, oiling the wheels of London's economy and opening up and regenerating the backlands of the capital. An earlier precursor of the JLE was known as the River Line. The title could well be applied to what has been built during the 1990s. The JLE follows the curves of the Thames, from Wordsworth's Westminster Bridge, through the Bankside of Chaucer and Shakespeare, past London Bridge, into the former docklands, and crosses the water to pursue the River Lea into the old East End capital, and new East End development focus, of Stratford. The line is the strongest reaffirmation possible that Richard Rogers is right and that the future of London rests with the river. Certainly, the river is the place to see the best of London's new millennium architecture – Michael Hopkins' parliamentary extension; Barfield & Marks' great London Eye ferris wheel; Rick Mather's impending renewal of the South Bank; Bryan Avery's IMAX cinema; the expanding community around Coin Street; Herzog & de Meuron's Bankside Tate Modern (with its bridge link to the City by Norman Foster, who is also extending London Bridge City); the new towers by Foster and Pelli at Canary Wharf; and the Rogers-designed Millennium Dome, with a new residential quarter growing around it. These can be dismissed as

The London Eye and Tate Modern are two of the new developments opened on the South Bank to celebrate the Millennium – they are markers of regeneration and are served by the Jubilee Line.

monumental gestures, yet they are just
products of an in-depth regeneration
process that is affecting not only the
riverside but Elephant & Castle (once
'the Piccadilly Circus of South London')
and Stratford Broadway too. It is not
so long since London Bridge was a
point of transition between City
wealth and South London shabbiness
– now Borough High Street is set to
become smart, even chic. One of the
most striking new restaurants in
London, Fish, nestles close to
Southwark Cathedral. The wealth of
London is spreading southwards and
eastwards. The JLE is moving it on.
London's last new tube line, the
Victoria Line, was a link between
mainline termini and the West End.
The JLE is a line of interconnections,
as important to wide swathes of the
East End, Kent and Essex as it is to
central London.

In the inter-war years, the
Underground created virtually new
areas of London and imposed on raw
suburban avenues, cut out of farmland
in North London's Edgware and Pinner,
the cachet of being a part of the
capital – the London Transport roundel
was a potent symbol of unity and
dynamic growth. The JLE, in contrast,
is an engine not for expansion but for
rediscovery. The television presenter
Dan Farson claimed that 'the history
of the East End was short-lived' – it
began with the construction of the
docks, but by the 1970s it was all but
over.[2] That judgement may turn out to
be very premature: there were once
Jeremiahs who claimed that people
would never commute from places as
distant as Finchley and Edgware.

The initial publicization of the
designs of the JLE stations back in
1991 acted as an inspiration for urban
metro and light railway systems in the
vanguard. Paris' Météor Line – eight
stations and a running length of 7
kilometres (4 miles), constructed partly
by tunnelling and partly by cut-and-

cover techniques – has produced striking daylit stations, such as that by Bernard Kohn at the Gare de Lyon or Grumbach & Schall's station serving the new Bibliothèque Nationale. Munich's metro has been extended to an overall architectural master plan, but with individual stations tackled by a variety of practices.

With its riverside route and very diverse physical context, the Météor Line has strong engineering parallels with the JLE. Architecturally, however, it is far less ambitious. Public transport is, by its very nature, about standardization: trains, track, signalling, signage and station equipment, from ticket machines to escalators, must be uniform linewide, if not throughout the system. The architectural programme of the JLE had its origins in the Hong Kong metro, British-designed and built. The Hong Kong stations, consistently uniform and spacious, were distinguished only by the remarkable use of overall colour to give single-colour stations – blue, yellow, and so on. What is special about the JLE is that the common theme in the stations, taking its cue from Hong Kong, moves from the use of colour to sculpted engineering solutions, as a starting point for a brilliant array of variations.

Roland Paoletti was schooled in concrete and structures under the great Italian engineer Pier Luigi Nervi in Rome, and as a transport architect in Hong Kong. While the Hong Kong passenger space standards were adopted for the JLE, it is undoubtedly Nervi's influence on Paoletti that has had the greater effect on the JLE. Nevertheless, Paoletti is adamant that his single aim was to produce a project rooted in 'London style', with stations designed by London architects given free rein to produce individual designs responding to London's highly varied neighbourhoods. Some of them –

Waterloo and London Bridge pre-eminently – are reworkings of 'discovered' space within older structures. Others – Canada Water or Stratford – are new London monuments, setting their stamp on whole quarters of the capital.

Paoletti discovered quickly that the Pick/Holden era was regarded as the golden age of the Underground. It had been conveniently forgotten that Pick himself was disappointed at the outcome of his efforts, considering even Sudbury Town station a 'botched' job: 'There is an entire lack of design and orderly worksmanship', he wrote, after seeing the clutter of fittings and equipment imposed on the new building.[3] The comment may strike a chord with some of Holden's successors. The changing technical needs of a transport system are often at odds with the 'orderly' environment that Pick wanted – as Paoletti recognized. Some of the architects commissioned to work on the JLE were apprehensive of the possible conflict between engineering – civil engineering, moreover – and architectural priorities. Had there been a rigid division of responsibilities, with engineers designing structures and architects fitting them out, the conflict would have been minimized, but the results would not have been architecture. What is special about the line is the degree to which architecture, as well as engineering, has been allowed to shape the stations, not just ornament them, without detracting from the essentially functional and operational brief given to the engineers. Never before on the London Underground had architects been given this licence to re-invent, nor were there any clear precedents from systems outside Britain.

In 1990, in fact, when the JLE's architectural commissioning process began, London Underground was widely perceived as being in a state of crisis, underfunded, decaying and even dangerous: the King's Cross fire had enormous impact. Critics of the JLE argue that the project further impoverished the Underground, diverting funds from much-needed improvements to other lines. Yet the Underground can never be the same after the JLE: it should be the harbinger for the renaissance of the whole system. 'We want people to complain about the state of the Underground', says Denis Tunnicliffe, looking forward to the reconstruction of major interchanges like King's Cross and Victoria, which now seem hugely inadequate alongside the rebuilt London Bridge and Waterloo. It was thanks to the adamant refusal of Wilfred Newton and Denis Tunnicliffe to cut the basic specification of the JLE, making the stations smaller, with fewer escalators and lifts, that it became a line to the future. 'The problem with most of our older stations is that the basic boxes are far too small', says Tunnicliffe.

The ethos of the Underground in pre-JLE times was of an institution living off its past. 'We are still slaves to graphics', says Denis Tunnicliffe. 'Edward Johnston's lettering is religiously protected, the roundel revered'. But the architectural legacy of Frank Pick has been put in its proper place – in the history of British architecture between the wars. In retrospect, the Victoria Line was the last expression of the old philosophy that design should be subjugated to operational imperatives.

Andrew Saint has brilliantly summarized the new London of the JLE as '...fragmented, robust and individualistic... youthful, raw at the centre, uneven on the edges...'[4] It is not the London that Frank Pick, an Arts and Crafts puritan at heart, would have recognized or countenanced. Yet it is reality. The JLE was never conceived as a millennium project –

back in 1990, it was scheduled to be completed within four years – but it has opened on the verge of the new century. It is not only London's greatest construction project, but that which expresses the confidence and verve of the millennium capital. The engineering achievement has been vast, the political and negotiating skills involved have been used to admirable effect, but it is for its architecture that the JLE will be remembered. Not since the Festival of Britain have outstanding British architects of the younger generation enjoyed such concentrated patronage. The 1951 Skylon, designed by Philip Powell and Hidalgo Moya, then barely out of the Architectural Association, is a potent symbol of London even today. The Festival was a temporary manifestation. The JLE is here to stay, a cross-section through the best of British architecture in the 1990s. Perhaps the greatest strength of its architectural programme is the refusal to impose an 'Underground style'. The Underground of the future, expressed in the JLE, is not a place apart, but a layer in the fabric of London, no longer to be avoided but to be admired and enjoyed. It marks the rebirth of public architecture in Britain.

Notes

1 Richard Rogers and Mark Fisher, *A New London* (London 1992), p. xl.

2 Dan Farson, *Limehouse Days* (London 1991), p.1.

3 quoted in C. Barman, *The Man who built London Transport* (Newton Abbot 1979), p. 138.

4 Saint, *op.cit.*, *Rassegna* 66 (1996), p. 32.

above
Bryan Avery's IMAX cinema near Waterloo has become a focal point for a previously undistinguished area.

opposite
The Jubilee Line Extension project predated Paris's Météor Line, where stations such as that serving the new Bibliothèque Nationale were similarly allotted to a number of architectural practices.

below
The campaign of regeneration and renewal along the route of the JLE finally realizes the vision implicit in the 1951 Festival of Britain.

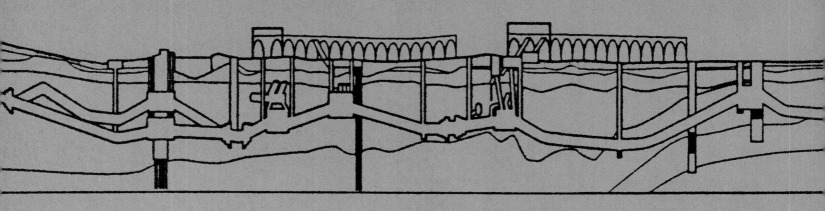

tunnelling
the line

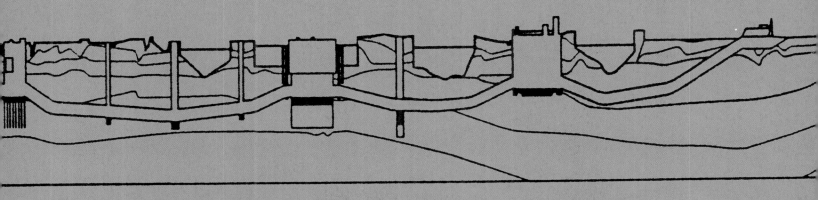

Anyone who has been down a tunnel under construction never forgets it. The steamy atmosphere and stygian gloom makes it difficult to envisage the transformation into a modern rapid transit railway. A tour of the massive caverns being constructed for the Jubilee Line Extension under London Bridge in 1996 would have provided a graphic illustration of just how far tunnelling techniques have advanced in the last 150 years.

The first real engineered tunnel in the world was Marc Brunel's Thames Tunnel, completed in 1843. Brunel's innovatory breakthrough was to invent the tunnelling shield – a device to protect miners and support the ground until a permanent tunnel lining could be built. This tunnel – all the more remarkable for being underwater – now carries the Underground's East London Line under the river southwards to a new interchange with the Jubilee Line at Canada Water. Modern bored tunnelling is still based on the same method employed by Brunel although the 'shields' are now technologically advanced and automated. In essence, the shield supports a short length of the ground while the sub-soil is excavated. The shield is then moved forward by pushing off the completed lining behind and another section of lining placed in the gap that is left. This cycle of operations continues until the tunnel is eventually completed. The operation is relatively straightforward in London Clay, which is 'self supporting' to an extent, but is much more difficult in water-bearing sands and gravels.

The London Underground network consists of two basic systems – the sub-surface lines such as the District, with shallow cut-and-cover tunnels and the tube lines such as the Northern and Jubilee with deeper, smaller tunnels. The tube tunnels have been formed by boring through the

previous pages
A geographical section of the JLE route.

left, from top
The central concourse tunnel at London Bridge Station in 1996 (top) and 1997 (second from top).

Brunel's Thames Tunnel after being taken over for use by the East London Railway.

Tube railway construction using a Greathead shield in October 1923.

opposite
Tunnel at Southwark Station showing the pre-cast concrete lining, April 1996.

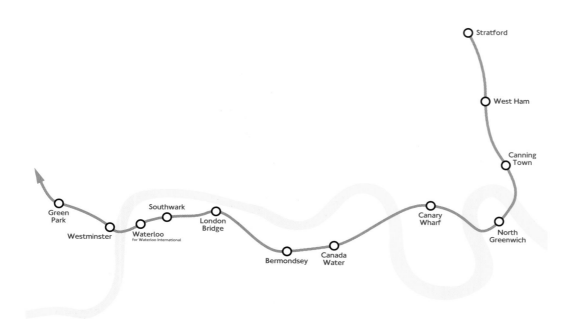

Route plan of the Jubilee Line Extension: the line crosses the Thames four times.

The site plan of Westminster shows the proximity of the station to Big Ben and other important buildings.

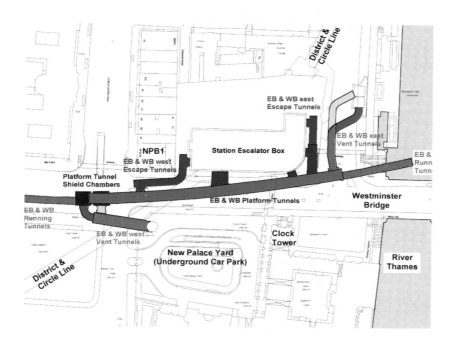

ground – the London Clay that lies under most of the capital is an ideal medium for tunnelling. South-east London is different in that most of the sub-soil is made up of waterlogged sand and gravels – much more difficult to tunnel through – which may explain why, with the exception of the Northern line, the 'tube' has not historically ventured into South and South-east London.

The first electrified tube railway was opened in London in 1890. This was the City and South London Railway, the forerunner of today's Northern Line. The running tunnels were only 3 metres (10 feet) in diameter and were constructed using Greathead shields (named for the builder of the Tower Subway) and iron segments, a method used, essentially unchanged, to construct most of London's tube network up to the end of the Second World War.

Following completion of the Victoria Line in 1968, longstanding plans for a new tube line into south-east London were dusted off and the Fleet Line, subsequently renamed the Jubilee Line, was born. The line stopped at Charing Cross when funding ran out in 1979, but by the late 1980s the rapid pace of development in Docklands meant that a new rapid transit link could not be put off any further and the go-ahead was given for an extension to the Jubilee Line which would run through South-east and East London to Stratford. By this time, the techniques for tunnelling through water-bearing ground had become much more sophisticated, capitalizing on the experiences of the Channel Tunnel and in the Far East.

Building a new underground railway posed many challenges. When the JLE was launched, 10 years had passed since the last tubes had been tunnelled through central London. In this decade, safety and environmental requirements had become more stringent and opposition from property and land owners along the chosen route was anticipated. Some key design criteria needed to be met – for example, avoiding sharp curves in order to maximize train speeds – and it was decided that the 'classic' tube railway profile would be adopted whereby each station is located on a hump to aid acceleration and deceleration of the trains. The tunnels then needed to be threaded through or past physical obstructions – including other tube railway and similar deep-level tunnels and the deep foundations of high-rise buildings. Finally, ground conditions needed to be taken into account, since tunnelling through 'bad ground' is more risky and expensive. Consequently, as much of the tunnelling as possible needed to be kept within the London Clay strata.

Once the problem of the alignment was resolved, the size of the various tunnels had to be determined. It was decided from the start that the new stations on the JLE would be much more spacious than ever before, necessitating much bigger excavations, particularly at the main interchange stations of Waterloo and London Bridge. At 4.35 metres (14 feet) in diameter, the running tunnels would also be larger than the then standard tube tunnels. The new size was big enough to incorporate a side walkway at track level for emergency access.

Consideration then turned to the most suitable tunnelling techniques. The route of the JLE, particularly between Green Park and London Bridge, was under or close to many important and historic structures – not least the Palace of Westminster and Big Ben. Between Waterloo and east of London Bridge, the JLE runs directly below the viaduct carrying main line and suburban trains into Charing

Cross, Blackfriars and Cannon Street. Any problems here could cause unthinkable disruption to thousands of commuters' journeys. On the plus side, all tunnelling as far as London Bridge would be through London Clay, enabling the use of traditional open-face shields. Once past London Bridge, tunnelling would be in water-bearing ground, requiring a very different approach. Traditionally, this type of ground has required the use of compressed air to support the face of the tunnel. However, because this is expensive and potentially hazardous to the health, tunnellers will always seek to avoid using it if possible.

To counter this, and in anticipation of the construction of the original Fleet Line, a new type of tunnelling shield had been prototyped at New Cross in 1972. Known as the bentonite slurry shield, this device held up the earth by using a bulkhead inside the shield body – enabling the miners to work at normal atmospheric pressure. Development of the slurry shield and, subsequently, the earth pressure balance machine was spearheaded by the Japanese. These types of shields are known as closed-face machines to distinguish them from the traditional open-face types where the miners are literally in contact with the ground being excavated.

It was decided at an early stage that tunnel lining rings would be either cast spheroidal graphite iron (SGI) or reinforced precast concrete. The precast lining segments would be either bolted together or, in the London Clay, simply 'expanded' into position. The SGI linings are particularly important where openings and connections between different tunnels have to be formed and for the construction of step plate junctions. A step plate junction is where one track diverges into two – such as at the junction with the existing line south of Green Park. The junction is formed of

left, from top
The Earth Pressure Balance tunnelling machine being lowered into the shaft at Bermondsey.

A train passing through the completed step plate at Green Park, January 1997.

A view of the triple escalator tunnel at Waterloo, showing the connection to the concourse, March 1997.

Permanent tunnel lining under construction at Jubilee Gardens, Westminster, October 1996.

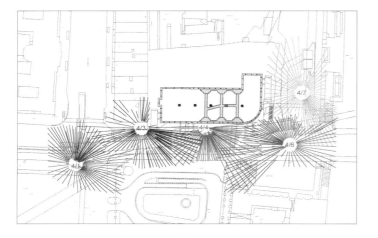

progressively increasing sizes of tunnel with a step between each section – hence the term step plate. To add to the engineering challenge, the step plates at Green Park were built without disrupting service on the existing Jubilee Line. This was done by building the new tunnel sections around the existing tunnel, temporarily supported as necessary, then finally dismantling the old rings before installing the new trackwork over a weekend. This method had been used several times before on the Underground, including the Victoria Line and the first section of the new Jubilee Line in the 1970s.

For the Jubilee Line Extension stations, it became clear that the platform tunnels and main circulating areas would need to be much larger than in the past to accommodate anticipated passenger numbers and to meet significantly higher safety standards. The stations at Waterloo and London Bridge posed particularly difficult problems owing to the rabbit warren of tunnels and underground and surface structures already existing – around and through which the JLE would have to be threaded. At Waterloo, for example, the new intermediate concourse is 10 metres (33 feet) in diameter while the escalator shafts containing three escalators are 8 metres (26 feet) in diameter. The limited amount of ground left after the tunnels were formed called for extensive ground treatment works to minimize settlement and damage. The so-called New Austrian Tunnelling Method (NATM) became a strong contender for tunnelling in the London Clay after trials were carried out at London Bridge.

NATM tunnels are formed using a reinforced sprayed concrete lining (also known as shotcrete). This method was first adopted for soft-ground urban use during the building of the Frankfurt Metro in 1968. Unlike bored tunnelling – where the whole tunnel cross section is excavated and lined incrementally using a shield to support the ground temporarily – NATM sets out to use the inherent strength of the ground itself as much as possible. Lattice girders, wire mesh and shotcrete are used in combination to provide initial support until the self-supporting equilibrium of the ground can be re-established. The tunnel cross-section is excavated in several 'bites' by digging out headings, each of which are temporarily supported until they are all joined together to form the whole tunnel. Finally, some form of permanent lining is installed in a follow-up operation.

The advantages of NATM, which was used to build the two huge crossover caverns for the Channel Tunnel, are that it uses relatively cheap materials and economic excavation methods. Furthermore, the permanent lining can also be of sprayed concrete or an in-situ reinforced concrete finish, much more economical than using iron or concrete segments.

The stage was set to make maximum use of NATM on the JLE and design and specification proceeded on this basis. However, the collapse of NATM tunnels being built at Heathrow for the Express rail link in October 1994 brought JLE work to a halt. There could be no further use of this method until LUL and the Health and Safety Executive were satisfied that any risks had been contained and that there was a clear understanding of what had gone wrong at Heathrow. To counter the delays, LUL decided to revert to traditional bored tunnel construction and this was used in some locations. However, the go-ahead to resume using the NATM method was given in early 1995 and significant amounts of the tunnels at London Bridge and Waterloo were constructed using this without any problem.

With more and more of the ground being removed from underneath London, sophisticated measures were required to prevent settlement and damage to overlying structures. The fact that modern Underground railway construction may require some 25 per cent of the ground to be removed over the station area at tunnel level indicates the size of the problem. Predicted settlement is often in the region of 150mm (6 inches) and preventing this scale of movement is the difference between success and failure.

To achieve this, the JLE employed extensive compensation grouting – a technique used to limit or compensate for the ground losses resulting from tunnelling works. In this expensive but essential technique a bentonite/ cement grout is injected into the ground under pressure in advance of, during and after the tunnelling works, ensuring that if any settlement does occur, further controlled injections of grout have a direct and immediate compensating effect. Steel or plastic tubes are inserted into the ground through which the grout is injected. Repeated injections can be made as tunnelling proceeds, in effect making the ground over the tunnel act as a hydraulic jack.

Compensation grouting proved very successful on the JLE, no more so than at Westminster where the new tunnels are within metres of the Palace of Westminster and Big Ben (92 metres/300 feet high and around 8500 tonnes), the foundations of which are around 10 metres (33 feet) above the top of the new eastbound Jubilee Line tunnel. A compensation grouting regime was developed and installed from purpose-built shafts in the vicinity, and was very successful in minimizing any further settlement and damage to Big Ben, with movement able to be controlled within a tolerance of 1mm.

The tunnelling of the JLE has been a major success story with over 25 kilometres (15 miles) of new tunnels formed below the heart of the capital and through the treacherous soils of South-east London, including four river crossings together with new junctions with the existing railway at Green Park. That this has been achieved without any fatalities or serious accidents is a tribute to the skills of the people employed in this endeavour and a lasting reminder of what can be achieved using the variety of constantly developing tools and techniques now available. Visiting London Bridge Station today will reveal how the underworld has been transformed into the Underground of the twenty-first century.

Bob Mitchell
General Manager,
Jubilee Line Extension Project

Notes

L.T.C. Rolt, *Isambard Kingdom Brunel* (1972)

D.F. Croome and A.A. Jackson, *Rails Through the Clay* (1993)

W.J. Rankin, 'Recent developments in compensation grouting' in *Tunnels and Tunnelling*, May 1996

G. Sauer, *NATM in Soft Ground* (internet)

project credits

Westminster

architect: Michael Hopkins & Partners
project team: Michael Hopkins, John Pringle, David Selby, Patrick Nee, Arif Mehmood, Annabel Hollick, Gail Halvorsen, Margaret Leong, Amir Sanei, Niels Jonkhans, Alexandra Small, Taro Tsruata, Toby Birtwhistle, Gordon McKenzie, Emma Adams, Ian Milne, Georgina Hall, Geoff Whittaker, Gina Raimi, Rebecca Chipchase, Hannah Wooller
JLE architect: Sui-Te Wu, Costas Hadjipiries
qs: Gardiner & Theobald
civils/structure: G Maunsell & Ptnrs
services: JLE
acoustics: Arup Acoustics;
fire: Arup R&D
lighting: George Sexton Assocs
contractor: Balfour Beatty Amec.

Waterloo

architect: JLE Architects
project architect: Sui-Te Wu (1992–99), Ian McArdle (1991–92);
design team: Andreas Gyarfas, Simon Moore (station architects 1990–92), Simon Fraser, Mark Ansell, George Novakovic, Ian Catchpole, Graham Gilmour, Howard Carter, Anthony Leslie, John Toovey, Leslie Beilby-Tipping, Chris Pound, Philip Bowen, Ian McLeod, Tony Joy, Luz Vargas, Simon Dickenson, Mark Bagguley, Julian Maynard, Clive Hogben, Stash Kelpacki, Marisa Holland
civil engineer: G Maunsell & Ptnrs
structural engineer: Brian Cole
services engineer: JLE Project Team
lighting: Barrie Wilde
acoustics: Arup Acoustics, Tim Smith
main contactor: Balfour Beatty Amec jv.

Southwark

architect: MacCormac Jamieson Prichard
project architects: Richard MacCormac, Freddy McBride
project team: John Attwood, David Bonta, Alice Brown, Helen Brunskill, Stephen Coomber, Matthew Dean, Dil Green, Pete Hull, Peter Jamieson, Martin Kehoe, Peter Liddell, Ian Logan, Chris McCarthy, Claire Mellor, Phil Naylor, Chris Schulte, Chris Scott, Morag Tai, Eddie Taylor, Christian Uhi, Simon Whiting
JLE architects: Andrew Henderson, Simon Moore, Tony Windmill
structural engineer: LG Mouchel & Partners
civil and structural engineer: Babtie DHV jv
qs: RWS Services, Mouchel Management
site contractor: O'Rourke Civil Engineering
lighting: Maurice Brill, Drake & Scull
cone wall: Adams Kara Taylor, Alex Beleschenko
contractor: Aoki Soletanche jv.

London Bridge

architect: Weston Williamson, JLE Architects
Weston Williamson project team: Bob Atwal, Stephen Bedford, Robert Bochel, Graham Fairley, Russell Gilchrist, Michael Haste, Steve Humphreys, John Jennings, Make Kuwayama, David Miller, Andrew Weston, Geoff Whittaker, Chris Williamson, Robert Elliston, Josh Wilson, Desmond Lavery, Chris Todhunter, Peter Duby, Stephen Bickler
JLE project team: Mashood Ahmed (project architect), Martin Short, Nigel Maynard, Peter Boyle (station architects), Debra Johnson, Ira Fazin, Reinne Elliot, Russell McDowell, Amrit Ambasna, Farked Fayed
structural design: Mott McDonald
contractor: Costain Taylor Woodrow jv.

Bermondsey

architect: Ian Ritchie Architects
project architect: Gordon Talbot
project team: Phil Coffey, John Comparelli, Simon Conolly, James de Soyres, Toby Edwards, Christopher Hill, Mark Innes, Toke Kharmpej, Ian Montgomerie, Raita Nakajima, Henning Rambow, Ian Ritchie, Paul Simovic, Anthony Summers;
JLE architect: Gordon Swapp, Russell Hayden, Judy Slater, Tina Tang
civil engineer: Sir William Halcrow & Partners
qs: Hanscomb Partnership
lighting: Lighting Design Vienna
acoustic: Phil Gillieron
structure: Ove Arup & Partners
landscape: Charlie Funke Assocs
contractor: Aoki Soletanche jv, O'Rourke Civil Engineering.

Canada Water Bus Station

architect: Eva Jiricna Architects
project architect: Duncan Webster
project team: Eva Jiricna, Christopher Mascall, Geoffrey Whittaker
structural engineer: Benaim Works jv
mechanical engineer: Furness Green & Partners
qs: George Corderoy
lighting: Lighting Design Partnership
acoustics: Tim Smith Acoustics
air quality: Aspinwall
traffic: Stuart Michael Assocs
geotechnical: Richard Davies Assocs
contractor: Carillion.

Canada Water Underground Station

JLE Project architects (1991–9):
Stephen Wright, Chris Todhunter
(project architects), Vivian Cummins,
Deidre Lennon, Robert Birbeck,
Robert Dowling, Phil Seaward, Tara Breen,
Desmond Lavery, Alan McGuire,
Nicolas Shaw, Robert Wood, Tony Joy,
Andrew Green, Neil Pusey, Liz Laywood,
Kathrine Willis, Michael Magnall,
Mark Williams, Stevan Bickler,
Colleen Yuen, Ali Ghotbi, Deborah Alan
architect (until 1993): Herron Associates
structural design: Benaim Works jv,
Buro Happold (glazed drum)
main contractor: Carillion.

Canary Wharf

JLE Project architect: Jerzy Lachowicz,
Simon Wing, Deidre Lennon, Simon Timms
architect: Foster & Partners
Foster & Partners project team:
Norman Foster, David Nelson, Gerard
Evenden, Rodney Uren, Richard Hawkins,
Ross Palmer, David Crossthwaite,
Armstrong Yakubu, Chris Connell,
Toby Blunt, Charles Diamond, Glenis Fan,
Lulie Fisher, Mike Greville, Lee Hallman,
Caroline Hislop, Eddie Lamptey, Stuart
Latham, Muir Livingstone, Niall Monaghan,
James Risebero, Danny Shaw, Tim Shennan
civils: Posford Duvivier, De Leau Chadwick
m&e: JLE
structure: Ove Arup & Partners
lighting: Claude Engle
landscape: Land Use Constultants
qs: DLE
contractor: Tarmac Bachy jv.

North Greenwich Underground

JLE Project architects (1991–9):
Richard Brown, Kevin Lewendon,
Simon Dickason, Luz Vargas, Shaun Russell,
Laura Kidd, John Bailey, Guy Marriage,
Colin Bennie, John Malig, Tsi Tsung,
Clive Powell, Luke Baker, Sven Steiner,
Iftikar Khan, Mark Lechini, José Aguilar-
García, Anthony Leslie, Derek Clarke,
Ken Taylor, Paul Allen, Nick Harrop,
Denis Jordaan, Marisha Holland
architect (1991–4): Alsop Lyall & Störmer
(now Alsop & Störmer and John Lyall
Architects, respectively)
project team: Will Alsop, John Lyall,
John Smith, Jonathan Adams
engineer: Benaim Works jv
m&e: Drake & Scull
contractor: McAlpine, Wayss & Freytag,
Bachy jv.

North Greenwich Bus Station

architect: Foster & Partners
project team: Norman Foster,
David Nelson, Robert McFarlane,
David Summerfield, Russell Hales,
Hannah Lehmann, Daniel Parker,
Clive Powell, James Risebro
project manager: LUL/Capital
Project Consultancy
structure: Anthony Hunt Assocs
services: Max Fordham & Partners
qs: MDA
landscape: Land Use Consultants
lighting: Claude Engle
contractor: Sisk & Son.

Canning Town

JLE Project architects: Frank Peacock,
Ewan McLean, Mark Ansell,
Julian Robinson, Richard Aylesbury,
José Aguilar-García, Ashley Dunn,
Colin Bennie, Mike Healey
architect: John McAslan & Partners
(formerly Troughton McAslan)
project team: Christopher Egret,
Nick Eldridge, Adrian Friend, Yasser el
Gabry, Hans Grabowski, Martin Harris,
Kevin Lloyd, Catherine Martin,
John McAslan, Christopher Mascall,
Greg McLean, Michael Pike, Raj Rooprai,
Piers Smerin, Jamie Troughton, Roger Wu
engineer: WSP Group
qs: EC Harris
contractor: Mowlem Civil Engineering.

West Ham

architect: van Heyningen & Haward
project team: Birkin Haward, Joanna van
Heyningen, Robin Mallalieu, Lucy Marston,
Bert Rozeman, Peter Williams
JLE architects: Ewan McLean,
Frank Peacock, Mike Healey,
Richard Aylesbury, Julian Robinson
technical contractor,
structural engineer: Kenchington Ford
qs: EC Harris
m&e engineer: JLE Project Team
structure: WSP
contractor: John Mowlem.

Stratford concourse

architect: Wilkinson Eyre Architects
(formerly Chris Wilkinson Architects)
project architect: Marc Barron
project team: Stafford Critchlow, Jim Eyre
(director), James Parkin, Vinny Patel,
Chris Poulton, Robert Troup, Oliver Tyler,
Chris Wilkinson, Geoff Turner
JLE architects: Ewan McLean, Frank
Peacock, Mike Healey, Richard Aylesbury,
Julian Robinson
structural, m&e/services engineer:
Hyder Consulting
civil engineer: Ove Arup & Partners
qs: Franklin & Andrews
environmental consultant: Loren Butt
contractor: Kvaerner Construction.

Stratford platforms

architect: John McAslan & Partners
(formerly Troughton McAslan)
team: Stephen Archer, Yasser el Gabry,
Martin Harris, Ken Hutt, David Medas,
John McAslan, Piers Smerin,
Jamie Troughton, Roger Wu
JLE team: Allen Ashcroft,
Richard Aylesbury
engineer: WSP Group
qs: EC Harris
contractor: Mowlem.

Stratford Market depot

architect: Wilkinson Eyre Architects
(formerly Chris Wilkinson Architects)
project architects: Simon Dodd,
James Edwards
project team: Paul Baker, Zoe Barber,
Dominic Bettison, Keith Brownlie,
Stafford Critchlow, Jim Eyre (director),
Stewart McGill, Nicola Smerin, Oliver Tyler,
Chris Wilkinson, Jonathan Woodroffe
structural engineer/qs:
Hyder Consulting Limited
m&e: Hurley Palmer Partnership
main contractor: John Laing Limited.

picture
credits

courtesy Bryan Avery: 195 top

courtesy Barfield & Marks: 193 top

Bridgeman Art Library: 60 top

E.C. Dixon: 22–3, 37, 39, 52, 88 top,
102–3, 182–3, 185, 187, 188 centre
and right, 189 left and centre, 198 second
from top, 201 top and bottom

Peter Durant/arcblue.com: 2, 50–51, 53,
54–5

courtesy Foster & Partners: 101, 115
bottom, 114–15, 193 bottom

Dennis Gilbert/View: 24, 26–7, 28–9,
34–6, 38, 40–43, 48–9, 56–7, 62–71,
76–83, 88 bottom, 89–91, 93, 96–7,
104–111, 116–117, 118 top, 122–3, 127–9,
134–6, 140–41, 146–7, 156–7, 160–7,
172–7

Guildhall Library/Corporation of London:
47 right, 86 bottom, 145 right, 154 top,
170 top

courtesy Michael Hopkins & Partners: 20

Hulton Getty: 21 top, 195 bottom,
198 third from top

Illustrated London News Picture Library:
33 bottom

JLE Project: 25, 33 top, 46–7, 60 bottom,
75 bottom, 86–7, 115 top (Graham Cook),
196–7

original watercolour by Duncan Lamb:
21 bottom, 32, 46 top, 61, 74, 87 top,
100 bottom

London Transport Museum: 11–15, 198
bottom

Mary Evans Picture Library: 114 bottom,
132 top

Museum in Docklands Project: 100 top

QA Photos: 178 (Jim Byrne), 198 top, 199,
201 centre

Timothy Soar Photography: 92, 94–5, 118
bottom–121, 124–6, 133, 137–9, 148–51,
158–9, 181, 184

Southwark Local Studies Library: 75 top

Troughton McAslan/JLE Project: 132

courtesy van Heyningen & Haward: 144–5,
188 top, 189 bottom

courtesy Wilkinson Eyre: 154–5, 170–71

L. Zylberman/Graphix: 194

index

author's acknowledgement

I am grateful to Laurence King for undertaking this book, to Philip Cooper of Calmann & King for progressing it, and to my editors, Jane Tobin and her successor, Liz Faber, for much painstaking work on seeing it through to publication.

All the architectural practices involved with the design of the stations have given freely of their time and I want to thank them for their generous help. The staff of the JLE project team, now disbanded, of London Underground Ltd., and of the London Transport Museum were equally helpful, as were a number of the project engineers, and I am particularly grateful to Denis Tunnicliffe for agreeing to be interviewed.

Roland Paoletti inspired this book and made the writing of it an education. No book can adequately record a project which will have far more impact on the future of London than any of those coming to fruition around the millennium. But I hope that something of its heroism and sheer quality – achieved against the background of an impoverished public domain and governmental indifference – emerges from these pages. Without Roland, the JLE would never have achieved those heights and this book is respectfully dedicated to him.

Kenneth Powell

publisher's acknowledgement

The publisher would like to thank everyone who contributed their time and expertise to the book, particularly Caroline Mallen, Bob Mitchell, Stephen Jolly, John Self, Julian Maynard and Sui-Te Wu at JLE; David Ellis and Sheila Taylor of the London Transport Museum; *Architecture Today* for assistance with project credits; Isambard Thomas for his continuing dedication; and of course Roland Paoletti for his enormous contribution.